D1250218

The Complete Guide to Buying at Garage, Yard, and Estate Sales and Selling Online for Fun and Profit

Dan Blakely

Copyright © 2017 Dan Blakely
All rights reserved.

ISBN: 0692828788
ISBN 13: 9780692828786
Library of Congress Control Number: 2016920566
Silver Sea Publishing, Pasadena, California

This book has been written for informational purposes only, and is not intended to provide, and should not be relied on for, tax, legal and business legalities. It is recommended you consult your own legal, tax, and business/accounting persons for such advice.

This book is dedicated to Joy, my friend, confidant, supporter, and cheerleader.

Table of Contents

Please Read This One Short Page First!

THE FIRST TWO chapters of this book, both chapter 1 and 2 are in word; BORING! The following chapters? Opposite, very EXCITING and easy to read! Because of this I was quite tempted to simply put those not so fun chapters at the end of the book instead of the beginning, obviously I did not.

Let's use an analogy as to why. Pretend someone was going to take you on a treasure hunt, let's say 100 or so miles off the coast of Florida. Now that person was EXTREMELY confident they know exactly where the shipwrecked treasure is, thus you would have no need to worry about finding the gold, silver and artifacts, for sure it's there. I'm guessing you would be quite excited to get to that spot and fast! However, you cannot. The vessel you are going to take needs to be prepared, supplies needs to be stocked and it cannot set sail until the weather is permitting.

This is kind of like garage sailing. I know where the treasures are! All but the first two chapters reference details as to both the where and the how to get your hands on it. It's pretty exciting! The first two chapters are simply preparing you for the excursion. That said, if you want to skip around and read a couple of the fun chapters first I say go for it! As I refer to in the preface, I would almost even encourage it! But please eventually come back to chapters one and two, they won't take that long to read and they are chock full of information on the preparation. They even have a "Safety" section, definitively read that.

So with that said; off you go!

Preface

I STARTED GOING to garage sales when I was a little kid. I was attracted to all the neat stuff that I had never seen before, and on a small allowance, I could buy things I could not otherwise have. I would subscribe to magazines about finding hidden treasures, but the only way I could afford to do that was to ride my bike to local sales; it was truly a treasure hunt.

But as life went on, so did responsibility. I retired at the young age of fifteen from my garage-, yard-, and estate-sale ventures. Decades later, after I had created a career, had a family almost on cruise control, and had weekends off, I decided to go back out and relive a little of my childhood. Though I met with some frustration at first because I had little idea of the value of things, I kept on attending. Then I started really utilizing eBay, which led me to see everything in a different light. I could find things for a few bucks that looked antique or vintage, bring them home, and discover if, indeed, I had found treasures—and treasures they often were. Sure, some things had little to no value, but I also found items that I paid a couple of bucks for that would sell on eBay for hundreds.

And it did not stop there. I experimented with other avenues of profit, such as selling books and CDs on Amazon. The list of potentials kept getting bigger. Here are just a few examples of real finds and profits:

Sold on eBay

Old, dirty, broken toy motorboat: paid $3.00
Sold on eBay for over $200.00
Broken Chicago Cubs bobber: paid $0.25
Sold on eBay for over $100.00
A shoe box full of old pens: paid $15.00
Sold for over $900.00
A few old hunter's wooden decoy ducks paid $200.00
Sold for over $1,500.00!

Sold on Amazon

All I did is list the items, mail them to Amazon, and wait for the credits into my bank account. Aside from inconsequential things like checking on my competition and reducing a price here and there, I did nothing from the minute I sent these to Amazon...nothing! Rounded-off figures as follows:

Harry Potter audio-book collection: paid $5.00, sold for $250.00
I was paid $205.00

Exchange & Production Economics book: paid $1.00, sold for 135.00
I was paid $110.00

The Forgotten Carols CD: paid $0.50, sold for $25.00
I was paid $18.00

Atlantis Crystal Chamber CD: paid $1.00, sold for $15.00
I was paid $10.00

Woven wire jewelry: paid $1.00, sold for $12.00
I was paid $7.00

(Do not underestimate the last few lower price sales. I put them there for a reason: they add up—and fast!)

Now I was beginning to look at everything from a new perspective. I was doing what I had loved to do as a child, but now I was making more than allowance money. Year after year, I discovered new ways to profit and new ways to enjoy reliving this wonderful hobby of attending garage, yard, and estate sales. For me personally garage sailing has always been more of a hobby than anything. Could I turn it into more of a business? Of course I could! But I have personally chosen to keep it as a fun hobby. You can do the same or you can go further, much further!

This book will give you all the ins and outs of things you should do, things you should not do, things you should buy, and things you should not buy. You may want to make a few extra hundred dollars a month, a thousand dollars a month or more. Perhaps you will desire to go in the direction of more of a full-time business. Maybe your wish is to just have a fun new hobby. Whatever you choose, this book will teach you the ins and outs of the buying side of garage, yard and estate sales. Numerous books may tell you how to hold garage sales, but I found few that adequately and completely describe how to attend them for profit. The potential at many of these sales is hugely underestimated. In this book you can take advantage of decades of experience. Why can't you make some extra money? Maybe you just want to find salable books for next to nothing and sell them for a regular monthly income on Amazon, you can easily do that. Maybe you want to go further and get more into the antiques and collectibles part of sailing, or perhaps you want to do a little bit of everything. There is no limit to what treasures are out there just waiting to be found!

The fascinating part of this wonderful hobby is that it does not end with this book. You may find a genre or even multiple genres or avenues of interest that well exceed the basics you may find here. In other words the sky is the limit! Pay special attention to the next section, "How to Use This Book," to help you learn which path you should take. I hope you enjoy your new hobby and venture and that it adds a dynamic to your life, as it has to mine.

Dan Blakely

Preliminary Thoughts and Ideas and How to Use This Book

I'M SURE THERE may be sections of this book you may choose to skip. Please do not let that be the next few pages about how to use this book. You will fare well by reading them, and they will make navigating your sailing excursions much more successful.

1. You do not have to read this book cover to cover; actually it's probably a good idea if you don't. Some of you may want to specialize in just one niche of buying and selling, or perhaps you might just want to learn how to jump on the book-selling bandwagon and make a nice profit on Amazon. This is a guide-book, and it will do just that: it will guide you through buying at garage, yard, and estate sales and reselling online for fun and profit. This is a very detailed and comprehensive book—as far as I know, one of the most if not the most complete on the market. That said, it can get a bit overwhelming if you try to digest the whole thing at one time. We are all unique, and different aspects of this hobby will attract people in different ways.

2. Read the table of contents first; look at the chapter titles and sections. Doing this will start to give you an idea on how you

are going to approach the information. You may find just one aspect of "garage sailing" that appeals to you. If that's the case, you may only need to read a few chapters. (Just don't skip the "Safety First" section in chapter 3.)

3. Be careful of chapter 2, "Organizing Your 'Office.'" It may overwhelm you to the point that you become discouraged. As I mention in that same chapter, it may be a good idea to get your feet wet before setting everything up. This method will serve two purposes: it will give you a better idea of what part of your new venture you like, and it should also serve as proof that this really does work. Once you have that confidence, you can go back to chapter 2 and take it from there.

4. Always remember that I created this book not just to make you extra money but to add a fun dynamic to your life. Try to look at it not only as a business or hobby but also as a way to improve your enjoyment of life.

5. This book was written by an amateur for other amateurs. I am not an antique dealer. I do not do this for a living, yet I've still been able to make great profits and have fun, which proves you can do the same. My opinions are just that: opinions. And some of my definitions of certain things are just that: *my* definitions. But they are ones that have proven to work for me. If you are interested in only one or even a few particular aspects of buying and selling, this book will help you take that interest to a higher level.

6. I personally have only used eBay and Amazon, so that's what I will be referencing in this book. However, whatever auction house you choose to use, whether it's eBay, Amazon, others, or even a combination of many, just make sure you carefully read their rules and regulations, for example certain items may be prohibited to sell at their auction house. Further, things are constantly changing, so keep up with those changes, and do take advantage of their customer service; this can be quite helpful. Always be on the lookout for free advice

or recommendations. Check out the auction house's help centers, investigate a little, review discussion boards, and read blogs. There is plenty of advice available for you, everything from packaging an item to auction formats and more. There is no shortage of help available for you.

7. Know what you like and what you are good at. If you are into fashion and know more than the average person about quality clothes, you might want to focus on that market. You'll probably be the expert at that sale. Use your expertise. Maybe you know more about chinaware and cookware than just about anyone you know. Use that! There is an overabundance of kitchenware items out there. I personally know very little about such things and have chosen not to spend time learning about them or perusing the massive amounts of cookery items and utensils. It's just too much for me, and it would take up quite a bit of time. But most importantly, I am just not that interested in it. The list goes on. Find out what you like. If you enjoy something but don't know much about it, start learning. If you like something, you will excel. Here are just a few niches:

Antiques
Clothing (both vintage and new)
Pottery (one simple turn of the item may reveal a stamp from a rare manufacturer)
Art (every genre possible is out there)
Chinaware, cookware, and silverware
Christmas decorations
Vintage eight-track players, cassette players, and boom boxes
Vintage turntables, receivers, and eight-track and cassette players
Vintage computers and accessories (becoming very collectible!)

Tools (newer ones can be resold for a profit, and older ones can be valuable vintage items)
Sewing and knitting supplies
Toys
Glassware figurines
Vintage electronic games
Rare VHS tapes
DVDs
Books and CDs
(pay special attention to this avenue of profit)

The list is simply endless!

As a matter of fact, let's address the concept of lists for a moment. I've read all sorts of things online that list items to look for at sales. Although I would encourage you to research as much as possible, I want to make it very clear that giving you a list of items in this book would be like tearing a few pages out of the dictionary and telling you, "Here's pretty much all you need to know about the English language." It just makes no sense. Any list of items or niches that I can give you would only be examples; again the list is virtually endless.

I personally dabble in much of what I see potential value in as long as the size of the item or the time invested in listing it does not outweigh the return. If I turn a plate or piece of pottery over and see a manufacturer's name, I'll sometimes check it out to see if it's a rarity. I don't spend a lot of time on that, but perhaps you would want to. There are simply no rules. If I see a vintage novelty eight-track player, I'll grab it. I will sometimes pass on an ordinary eight-track player, but, again, vintage electronics are big. You can be a master of one or a jack-of-all-trades.

You may enjoy certain items and want to master selling them. There is simply no right or wrong answer. Though, I will tell you this:

books and CDs, which are common items, can be the bread, butter, and the dessert of your business. They're abundant, and finding them is like picking up loose cash on the ground. Other items might be a bit less abundant, but they do come up. And when they do, I'd love to see you be the one to land a huge profit.

1
Getting Started

Linguistics

FIRST, LET'S DEFINE some of the words we will use throughout this book. You are going to be driving around Saturdays in search of garage, yard, and estate sales.

Instead of referring to it this way, here's a shorter, easier, and much more fun way to say the same thing. On Saturday mornings you are going "garage sailing." Now you can tell your friends that weather permitting, you are going to spend Saturdays sailing! This is the appropriate time to tell you that unless your particular geographic area is different, Saturdays are without a doubt the best day to go out. Most sales are held on this day, and even though ads and signs may make reference that the sale is for Saturday *and* Sunday, that does not necessarily hold true. Often the sellers either sold an ample amount of items or are simply too worn out to extend it into Sunday. No matter what the signs or ads say, limit your outings to Saturdays only and you won't be sorry. But again, your geographical area may be different, so just feel it out a little.

In addition—and for purposes of keeping the feel of this book light and fun—we are going to often refer to this new venture of yours as a hobby, not so much as a business. The word *business* often conjures negative thoughts, in a similar manner to *work*. Just making these small changes in terminology will help your attitude in ways you can't imagine. It will make this journey of learning the process all the more enjoyable and successful.

We are going to refer to the sales you attend as *garage sales*, as opposed to *yard sales*. The terms really mean the same thing: people are selling their unwanted items, and even though a majority of them display their inventories in their yards, much of the items are probably from their garage, attic, and closets. Either term is fine, but for the purposes of this book, we'll just call them garage sales. Professional estate sales are a different animal altogether, which we will address in chapter 3.

Finally, as I stated earlier, although there are other auction houses out there, I personally only use eBay and Amazon, so those are the two we will be making reference to. Do check out other online auction houses if you are so inclined; you may want to explore what they have to offer.

Attitude

Any new life venture—whether it be a career change, new relationship, new home, new car, and so forth—may present a change in your life that results in apprehension and stress. Such feelings stem from how we react as human beings to change. But another feeling is mustered up during the course of new challenges: excitement! We are meant to grow in life rather than be complacent, which is evidenced by that invigorating energy we receive when we start a new project or venture that we're excited about.

Your viewing your new hobby of attending garage sales for fun and profit in a positive light is very important. See yourself having a great time; envision yourself learning and becoming fuller as a person with this added dimension in your life. The attitude you choose to adopt will make all the difference in the world as to whether this is going to work and—most importantly—whether it is going to be enjoyable for you. I have held off making any reference to the excitement of the money because there are so many other wonderful benefits, which in turn make the financial end even sweeter! One of the best feelings you can have is making money by doing something that you find fun and enjoyable. There's an old saying: "Won money is twice as sweet as earned money." In this sense, garage sailing is like gambling and winning but extremely safe. The question is not so much will you win but how much you'll win. Imagine sitting down at a slot machine and knowing that almost every time you pull that lever (I'm dating myself—really pushing that button), you will win something, and quite often it will be a nice amount. Such expectations should be felt for sailing. Yes, there will be losses every now and then, but they are so nominal that they are almost not worth mentioning.

You will continually learn a new skill that you can fine-tune more and more every week. You will begin to learn about the history behind certain items, things your parents, grandparents, and even great-grandparents used as parts of their daily lives. You will be introduced to new types of music, movies, and reading material. You will meet new people as you jump from one sale to the next. You will also interact with different types of individuals from all over the world with whom you will be dealing with as your buyers.

Many new and wonderful facets of your life will evolve from garage sailing. You will gain an additional income, money that was not available to you prior to reading this book. You can use the money for anything you want. You may desire to supplement your household payments, increase your wardrobe, or start a college fund for your children. You may just decide to go out to fancy restaurants or buy expensive seats at your local playhouse or concert venue. Maybe you will use the money to make car payments. Perhaps you will not spend a dime of your money and will decide instead to save it until you have enough to buy that Rolex watch you've been wanting all your life! No matter what you want to do with your money, it is important that you picture yourself spending it in the way you choose, and of course, in a way that brings *you* pleasure. The mind has a funny little habit of turning enjoyable visualizations into realities.

Sharing with the Family

Your family is also going to benefit from your involvement in sailing. I can just about guarantee that you will be in a better mood because you will have gained something that takes you away from some of the stress and monotony that daily life can sometimes throw at us. In addition, I have never seen people succumb to bad moods when they suddenly find extra money floating around. Your family and friends are going to be beneficiaries of your Saturday excursions.

When I am sailing, I always think about the people closest to me and the things they enjoy in life. If I see items at sales that I believe friends or family members may really appreciate and use, I'll buy them. I then get to enjoy the satisfaction of seeing their expressions when I present those hard-to-find items, which they can use in every-day life or add to their hobbies or collections. In addition, sometimes when I make a huge find, I celebrate by taking my family out to a very nice dinner.

Informing your family about your desire to go garage sailing and how much time it will take you away from them is essential. This is typically a nonissue because not much time is required to invest in sailing. All the same, you should present this information to your family or significant other just so you are all on the same page. Once they know exactly what you will be doing and how you will be happier because of it, I am confident they will become more than supportive of your ambitions. If they or you ever find that the hours you do spend are a challenge, then you may want to take a look at your daily life and see how else you spend your time. Is there something you can cut out that will allow more time for this new venture? How much television do you watch during the week? How much time do you spend on the Internet? Do you spend an exaggerated amount of time on your smartphone or texting? I have no doubt you could make a rather long list of things you do during your daily life that are not completely necessary or are even unhealthy in some ways.

Supplies

After you have adopted a positive attitude and have shared your plan with your family, you will then be in a position to start the next process. Any new venture must first start with a plan of action. Luckily, you do not have to develop a plan for yourself; I've already done that for you. What you do need to do, however, is put things in order so the plan will work. If you decided to build a tree house and had a book that showed you how to proceed, you would still need to visualize how the tree house was going to look before you made a move forward. Next, you would find the right-sized tree and one that would support the weight of the house. You would write down a list of the supplies you needed. Last, you would go to your nearest lumberyard and hardware store and buy those supplies. You would then, finally, be in a position to start the work on your castle in the branches.

Hopefully, I have managed to insert the first step of visualization into your mind. The second step of putting a list together has been done; you're holding it in your hand! Now all you have to do is implement the third step, and that is to go out on a garage-sailing supply-shopping spree.

A Consideration Prior to Purchasing Supplies

I suspect the majority of you are *not* going to want to spend a dime on supplies or take the time to purchase them because you're not quite sure if this garage-sailing thing is for you. There is nothing wrong with going out on a few Saturday excursions and hunting for your treasures *before* you commit to getting supplies. Once you feel confident, then you can go on your shopping spree. Either way is acceptable. Personally I would almost rather see you skip this section for now and go ahead and wait until you have gone out garage sailing, but don't wait too long. If you start building a big inventory too soon, you will find yourself only cluttering your room or office, all the while dying from impatience to get your items on the market. You really can't sell too many items before you have the supplies. Otherwise, when your inventory starts selling (and most of it will), you're going to feel rushed as you try to ship the purchased items, which results in more rushing to get supplies. Having said that, you can sell just a few items with a very limited amount of supplies. Some of you may want to do that before going full throttle on this, so either read on, or if you want to get your feet wet first before buying supplies, then go ahead and jump to the section in this chapter entitled "Are Garage Sales Seasonal?"

Where to Go

As you start garage sailing, you will actually find some of your supplies there for practically nothing—envelopes, tape, and so forth. I would also suggest that in the future, you keep an eye open for other sales, whether they are liquidation sales of some sort or just advertised promotions at your local office-supply store. In the meantime, however, you need to stock up now because you do not have the luxury to wait to find things at garage sales or even for one of the inventory liquidations.

I buy much of my supplies at one of the larger chain office supply stores. Depending on where you live, there should be an abundance of them out there. They really are one-stop shops, where you can find most—if not all—of your items at once. Also, join their free membership. They will mail or e-mail you promotions and coupons to keep you coming to their chain.

Purchase supplies that will last you a few months at minimum. Doing this will save you both time and money. You typically get better deals when you purchase in bulk, and I would rather see you using your valuable time doing other things as opposed to driving to the store every couple of weeks to buy more supplies.

Also, check out your local dollar stores. Sometimes they have a plethora of mailing supplies, but those supplies might not last long, or the stores might not get more. Buy what you can. If you are on a very limited budget, then just buy a little at a time. Once you've made a few sales, invest that money in a few months' worth of supplies before buying that beautiful sweater or golf club you've had your eyes on.

Another place you can purchase supplies is on the Internet, where you may find better prices; you'll also be saved the hassle of having to drive down to your local office-supply store. The only challenge is that right now you are charged, excited, and ready to go. I would hate to see you have to postpone that excitement until you've received your items in the mail. I would rather see you physically go out and buy the supplies for now, even if it is a few bucks more. In addition, you will actually be able to see the different kinds of items out there, and doing so will help you become familiar with the varied brands and prices.

What to Buy
I have provided an itemized checklist of the essentials that will be needed to successfully handle your new hobby. Most of the items are relatively inexpensive. In many other kinds of money-making opportunities—or most hobbies, for that matter—the supplies needed to start and maintain the venture are quite vast and may be extremely expensive. Think about getting into higher-end photography. Can you imagine the kind of money you would need to spend just to get started? It is quite the opposite with sailing: you probably have many of the necessary supplies somewhere in your house already. The following is an itemized list that covers what you need and why.

Computer, Smartphone, and Printer
The computer is a must-have. I will refrain from going into too much detail, because so few households are without at least one computer. If by chance you do not own one, you should utilize the know-how of someone who is familiar with computers and knows how to set them up. Finding an expert is easy to do; that someone could be a friend, relative, or work associate. It is not necessary to spend a fortune on purchasing a computer, so be careful. If you walk into a store but lack the relevant knowledge, you may end up buying much, much more

than you need. Start out as inexpensively as you can; you can always upgrade later if you choose. Laptops and tablets are completely acceptable; some of them even have cameras.

Camera

If you have a smartphone, laptop, or tablet with a camera, then that's all you need; otherwise, get a digital camera. Don't feel you need to spend a lot of money. You are not doing professional photography work. You are just taking pictures of your inventory items to help future buyers have an idea of what they are bidding on. I would, however, recommend that you get a camera that works well both out-doors and indoors. I had one camera that always made the item look either too dark or too light. I upgraded to another one that I bought secondhand, and it makes every item I sell look clear and sharp. Someone who knows about cameras should be able to lead you in the right direction.

Boxes

These do not have to cost you one dime. Just keep your eyes open for clean cardboard boxes of all sizes. If you receive something in the mail that comes in a box, just hang on to the box. When you are at a store, occasionally ask the manager if there are any old boxes in the back you can have. Just stay away from the produce and meat depart-ments; the last thing you want to do is mail something in a box with pieces of old vegetables, fruits, or meats stuck to the bottom. The customer wouldn't likely appreciate that. What's more, be careful with liquor-store boxes. The USPS for instance has rules about send-ing items in boxes that advertise alcohol, so ask your mailing house or check out their website for clarity on this or any other rules about packaging they might have.

   If you lack the time or inclination to obtain boxes using the sources mentioned above, you can always just buy them at your office-supply store, but they're not that cheap, relatively speaking. What I do is typically purchase ten packs of folded-up file boxes.

They are often referred to as banker-style boxes. You can fit a lot of different items into them, and they are very inexpensive yet sturdy. I only buy boxes when I've run out of the ones I've found. You will need boxes of every size imaginable. You may come across a tiny ring-size box or one big enough to hold a set of speakers—either way, grab them!

There is a way to acquire various sizes of sturdy boxes that are clean, unused, and made solely for mailing purposes, and this way won't cost any money. Where? The US Post Office. They will supply you with free boxes but only for the purpose of priority mailing. Head to your local post office, and ask a clerk for a few priority boxes of different sizes. The clerk should be more than happy to accommodate you and explain the rules or you can simply check online.

Tape
I do not mean masking tape or the kind of tape you use to wrap gifts. I am referring to heavy-duty tape for packaging and mailing purposes. The rolls are usually about two inches wide and often come in a package with multiple rolls, which is the best way to purchase them. Usually, a package comes with a free tape dispenser, which you can use repeatedly. You are going to be using a lot of tape, so grab several rolls. Keep in mind that the US Post Office may also give you priority tape for the packaging of priority items. Another good idea is to get a roll of brown packaging tape that is also two inches wide; however, you will not use this kind of tape often, so purchasing just one or two rolls is adequate. You will use this tape mostly for giving extra hold to unsightly seams, gaps, or small tears in your cardboard boxes. You can also use it to cover up old writing or labels on your boxes. You will not use it often, but it will come in handy.

White or Brown Wrapping Paper
You can purchase this in a roll just like gift-wrapping paper, except it's sturdier, more durable, and great for a number of purposes including wrapping boxes that will be sent thousands of miles.

You will often send an item in a box that was used for something else. For example, you may not want to send a collectible teddy bear in a box that is labeled for toilet paper! In a case like this, you can just wrap the box in brown wrapping paper and then write the address directly on it. Just make sure you secure the paper with lots of tape to keep it from tearing off. Remember, you are protecting not only the paper but also the address you wrote on it. If the paper gets ripped off, the "to" and "from" addresses disappear along with it, and your item may end up in the twilight zone of a post office. If you have a choice, it is better to write the addresses directly on the box or use a label.

You can also use the brown paper to wrap up an item that you have bubble wrapped. For instance, tennis racquets can be very annoying to mail because finding boxes that fit the sizes of these racquets is difficult. What I do is add two or three layers of Bubble Wrap to the racquet, then double wrap those layers with paper. Finally, for extra hold and protection, I wrap tape around it a few times. My adding so many layers creates a sturdy package, and I can do so very quickly, allowing me to avoid needless searching for right-sized boxes.

You can also put that wrapping paper in your boxes to keep the items from moving during deliveries. You can use those Styrofoam peanuts, but doing so gets a bit costly. If you really want to save a few bucks, just buy the Sunday newspaper and use it as filler inside your boxes. Shredded paper also works great.

Bubble Wrap
You can purchase this in a roll. I typically buy the roll that is 12 inches wide and 195 feet long, in a box. (The box it comes in is also a great size for storage or for sending bulky items.) You want to use Bubble Wrap for just about everything you send. It gives items quite a bit of protection and shows buyers that you care enough to safeguard their purchases. An interesting little side note is that everything looks more valuable and desirable when it comes wrapped in plastic wrap or Bubble Wrap! Buy both the thick and thinner kind and distinguish which size is appropriate for each item that you ship.

Envelopes

What I am referring to are padded or bubble mailers. Among other things, they are absolutely perfect for small odds and ends that are flatter in structure. Mainly, however, these envelopes are crucial for the packaging and mailing of DVDs and CDs, which you will be mailing often. You can even buy the larger padded envelopes when you need to send out multiple DVDs or CDs to a buyer. You will definitely want to purchase these envelopes in bulk. I strongly suggest you buy these online, because they are much less expensive when you purchase a bulk quantity. I usually buy three hundred to five hundred at a time, and—oh yes—keep the boxes they come in. They are typically good quality and perfect for many different kinds of items. Because mailing DVDs and CDs is so popular, these types of envelopes are actually advertised for that purpose. Knowing the measurements is unnecessary; just look for the following words in the advertisements: padded, bubble, and CD or DVD. For the time being, you should probably pick up fifty or so at your local office-supply or dollar store. Then, as I suggested earlier, start buying in bulk online.

Labels

Buy a package of labels for those times when, for whatever reason, you cannot write directly on the box or envelope. You won't need them often, but they're good to have just in case. They are simple mailing labels and have "from" and "to" spaces, along with enough room to write the addresses. Also, keep in mind that as with the priority boxes, a post office will gladly give you labels for priority mailing. In addition, eBay and Amazon have programs that supply labels for customers' shipments; customers only have to print the labels in those programs. Do whatever you are comfortable with. Often, I just print addresses on regular paper and simply tape them to the pertinent boxes or envelopes.

Plastic Protector Sheets

These are perfect when you have an item that, for whatever reason, you don't want to bubble wrap. An example would be a collectible magazine. Enclosing it in Bubble Wrap would be awkward, and you may end up bending it. Instead, you can simply insert it in one of these sheets, and you're good to go. They are also good, of course, for books. I typically purchase the size that will fit a *Life* magazine, about fifteen inches by eleven inches. You can buy a package of one hundred for very little, which will end up lasting quite a long time, depending on how often you send out magazines, books, and thin paper-like items.

Return-Address Stamp
Instead of taking the time to type or write out your return address on everything you send, if you are not using preprinted labels, go to your local office-supply store. They will make a self-inking stamp for very little. Using a stamp is easier and will last longer than you may assume; what's more, it's a great time-saver. The writing produced by stamps is more legible and easier to read for post offices and recipients, and it looks much more professional.

Plastic Shelving
This is the type of shelving that fits comfortably in a closet or against a wall. The type I've always used is approximately thirty-four inches long, fourteen inches deep, and fifty-four inches tall. It has four shelves, and I found it at one of those huge home stores. It is very inexpensive, takes about a half hour to put together, and is just a great organizing tool for my envelopes and other supplies. In chapter 2, we will go into more detail on how to best utilize this tool.

The following list covers miscellaneous office products that I feel are good to have at your disposal.

Tape Measure
When you describe your items, keep in mind that buyers will often want to know the measurements. I would advise you to buy a small tape measure, as the larger ones are unnecessary and clumsy. A

twelve-footer is just fine. Better yet just buy one at a garage sale; there are quite a few tape measures out there, so you will have no problem finding one.

Black Markers
Buy a package of fine-point permanent markers. They work well for handwriting addresses on boxes and envelopes. They are also good to use if you need to cross out labels or if you are writing on boxes.

Hand Sanitizer
You will touch all sorts of things during your sailing, some of which have been sitting in people's garages, attics, or what have you for decades. Just keep one of these bottles handy at your desk and in your car, along with a roll of paper towels, for when the need to clean your hands presents itself.

Insect Spray
Not often, but every now and again at the sale or after you get home, you may see a little "friend" in or around your finds, so have some insect spray on hand.

Scotty Peeler
This is a small plastic device used to help take stickers safely off books. You can get them online for less than five bucks.

Magnifying Glass
Get a powerful one, but don't feel as if you need to spend too much money. Get the kind with a dual magnifier (a magnifier within the main magnifier), and ideally one with a light. These added features will really help discern the tiniest details. A magnifying glass comes in handy for reading many things like worn and aged fine print on an antique or collectible or, perhaps, small printed copyright details or even a faded signature on an old book you find. I've found many books with someone's signature, and hey, sometimes that signature

might be the author's. Cha-ching! Such finds could be a big payday for you.

You should now have all the supplies necessary to move forward.

Are Garage Sales Seasonal?

Yes and no. Much may depend on your geographic location. As a rule, spring through summer is when you will likely find most sales. People are doing spring cleaning or moving, and the weather, especially during spring, is conducive for holding a garage sale. Right around September things will start slowing down and then more so into the holidays. The year will start off slow, and then come March things start picking up again. But watch out for the holiday weekends. If it's a major holiday I would recommend staying home, if however it's a lighter, more of a layback three day weekend then you might want to give it a go. You should also ask yourself if the last weekend or two had bad weather. If so perhaps there will be more garage sales even though it's a holiday weekend. If you end up wanting to give it a go and it's too slow you can always just come back home.

Now back to the off months, this does not in any way mean there will be no garage sales, it's just that you will not be putting the odds, or in this case, the numbers, in your favor. If you are so inclined, then sure, go out, but don't expect the quantity and quality of items you will find during the good months. Will you get lucky? Perhaps yes, you may, but I don't want to see you get frustrated, and the off months could very well take the wind out of your sails. But again, there is no hard-and-fast rule, so try going out a few times during the off season; perhaps your particular area will produce more garage sales then other areas.

Routing

People often ask me if I check the paper or online advertisements for where garage sales are going to be. My answer? Never. There's no need; there are plenty of garage sales out there, so why drive to just a few that were advertised? Why not put together a route? This way you'll come across all the sales, whether they are advertised or not, and I do believe the vast majority of garage sales are never advertised in the paper or online anyway.

Your geographic location will make a big difference on how you set up a route. You will really need to safely attend at least twenty plus garage sales in one Saturday. This truly is a numbers game. If you live in a smaller town, but experience has taught you that garage sales are abundant, just stay where you are. However, if there is no way you can hit the proper number of sales, you need to scout outside your area, perhaps in a nearby suburb. In that case, you need to leave your house earlier to be on your route by seven or eight in the morning. If you already live in a large suburban area, you're a bit ahead of the game. However, you still need to zero in on areas that will yield you the most profits. This may be a trial-and-error procedure, but if you take my advice, you will avoid not only quite a bit of hassle and frustration but will also increase your odds of success. The following are vital hints that will aid you in developing the best route possible for your nearby areas.

Expensive Areas
Although neighborhoods with expensive homes are more likely to have a greater number of valuable and higher-quality items for sale, they also have a few negatives. First, other people are thinking the exact same thing—that is, great deals are found at high-end garage sales. Now you have a problem with supply and demand: too many people are after the same few things. What is most important, however, is that although garage sales at expensive homes can be good despite the inevitable competition, the real problem is that there are fewer of them. I have focused on attending sales in only expensive areas, but I ran into a certain crucial problem: there were not that many sales. What's more, there was quite a bit of distance between the sales I did find.

Remember the numbers game? Attending garage sales in only high-end areas may yield you a better deal here and there, but because of the amount of time it takes to attend these sales—not to mention the competition—they are simply not worth focusing on. Stay away from expensive areas unless you have no choice than to drive through one to stay on your route. I actually did have an expensive area on my route, but I really had no choice. I was not going out of my way to attend them since I was already there because of the logistics of my area. When I drove through the high-end neighborhood and saw a garage sale, I ended up stopping, but I did not waste my valuable time to search for the expensive area. It just came across my path.

Low-Income Areas
These are the opposite of high-end areas. You will find numerous garage sales but also a few negatives along the way. In many cases, these garage sales are not a one-time thing for the proprietor. In low-income areas, there is a stronger likelihood that homeowners or renters are having regular sales because they are trying to supplement their household incomes. These are the worst kind of sales because, as I articulate in chapter 4, if the sellers' items do not sell, no big deal; they'll just put them out next week. This means they may ask far too much money for these items, leaving you without much leverage in your negotiations. Also, in low-income areas, you have poorer odds of finding higher-quality items that result in profitable acquisitions. Stay away from the low-income areas if you can, unless, like with the higher-end homes, you have to travel through them on your route anyway.

Middle-Income Areas
Here you go! Sometimes the middle of the road is best, and this concept proves true in garage sailing. That is not to say that you won't find favorable items in high-income or low-income areas; it's just that you lessen your chances of doing so. By focusing on middle-income areas, you will eliminate many of the problems that accompany

high-income and low-income neighborhoods. You will definitely find a higher volume of sales as opposed to high-income areas, and you will not see as many of the same people holding regular garage sales as you would in low-income neighborhoods. In middle-income areas, you will find good-quality items that will translate into strong profits when you resell them. Also, unlike high-end areas, the homes are closer together. If a street has a greater number of homes, more garage sales should be occurring, increasing your odds of finding resalable items, meaning more profit for you.

An important factor is the age of the homes. The older the area, the greater the odds are you will find in-demand antiques and vintage collectibles. That is not to say that you will not find good deals in newer neighborhoods; rather, it is simply more likely you will find older items in the older areas; it's just common sense. Do your best to stick with older homes. When I refer to older homes, I don't necessarily just mean from the turn of the century. Homes built thirty plus years ago or so can have a lot of vintage stuff as well as DVDs, CDs, books, and so forth. If you mix in some newer homes, that's okay. As with high- and low-end homes, if you find that you need to go through newer areas to stay on your chosen route, then do so. Why pass them up? Just try to focus on older areas when you plan your route, this is if you can.

If there are no older neighborhoods in your geographic location, just go to the newer areas. But even though you will still find other types of resalable merchandise in newer areas, focusing on older areas is the better path if there's a choice. Such areas simply raise your chances of success. However, newer homes, like many of the older homes, will still have newer resalable items as well as DVDs, CDs, and books, which will constitute a big portion of your profits.

Great! You have your route. You have committed it to paper and literally routed the best, safest, and fastest way to get to as many sales as possible. Now you have to test it. Spend a few Saturdays fine-tuning it. You may find that you are driving through too many commercial areas, which cuts into your time. Just tweak the route a little. After a few Saturdays, you will know if it's working for you. Once you have chosen a route that seems to work well, just stick with it, but if you still think you can do better with a revised route, give a new one a go. You can always return to your original route. One advantage of keeping the same route is that you will recognize the repeat garage sales and keep driving.

Setting Up Your Internet Account (Why I Use eBay and Amazon)
If you are computer savvy, this part of your hobby should be very easy for you. However, if your talents lie elsewhere, find someone who is good with computers and have him or her help you set up an account.

I use eBay and Amazon and have found them to be very user friendly when it comes to selling. I don't think it's any secret that eBay and Amazon are huge, well known, and respected companies that have revolutionized the way a large part of the world buys and sells. They are continually finding new ways to help people profit in their ventures. Most important, you would be hard pressed to find any individual who would not recognize the names Amazon and eBay; in other words, both companies have a huge market share of goodwill. You may still want to check around to find what other resale websites are out there. Personally, I've just stuck with the latter two.

Providing explanations on how to set up accounts and how to use them is another area I will not be addressing because accounts can be different and are constantly changing. In regard to online selling and marketing, I can tell you that there are many books on the market that will aid your online ventures by making them, among other things, more profitable. Although your referencing these other guides will increase your odds of success, I don't think they're necessary to get started. Amazon and eBay, as I mentioned earlier, make their systems very user friendly and are adept at helping educate you, the customer. The more you educate yourself, the more successful you'll be. However, it's not imperative that you read a bunch of books to make my systems work for you. Throughout this book, I will share some systems that I feel work very well and use often.

I have purposely made the next two sections, "Why I Use eBay" and "Why I use Amazon," as simple as possible; otherwise I fear you are going to get overwhelmed and frustrated. We don't want that to happen. Remember the key component to sailing? Fun!

Why I Use eBay (Do Check Out eBay's Rules and Regulations)
I use eBay for everything including bulk sales, which we will get into later in the book; however, with books and CDs, I mostly use Amazon. On eBay, I have my own account, and sellers hold me responsible. I make sure they are satisfied, and I do everything in my power to maintain a high-feedback rating; my doing so encourages other buyers to buy my stuff. On eBay—and this is crucial—I almost always list my rarer items in the auction format, items that may (and often do) drastically exceed any fixed prices I could have established. eBay does have fixed-price formats, and I typically use this for items that I am very confident will not exceed a certain price. We will be going into this in much more detail later in chapter 9, "Marketing Your Finds."

Why I Use Amazon (Do Check Out Amazon's Rules and Regulations)
I use Amazon for selling general non-collectible books and often CDs (see chapters 7 and 8). This in no way means you should not use Amazon for selling other items. I just personally like Amazon for selling books and CDs as fixed-price listings and eBay for everything else. On Amazon I establish certain prices that are competitive with other sellers, and my asking prices are what I will hopefully get if my items sell. Amazon has different ways to sell, however. One is the Merchant Fulfilled Network (MFN) format. This means you, as the seller (merchant), are taking care of everything—as you would in eBay. You list items, you deal with the buyers, you mail the items, and you handle

customer service. However, here's where Amazon gets really cool, and personally it's the only way I use Amazon. It offers something called Fulfilled by Amazon (FBA). You guessed it—Amazon fulfills the sale, mailing, and customer service, not you. Although anyone can buy your item, Amazon also has something called Amazon Prime membership; someone can pay a membership fee and get free expedited shipping. Members typically pay more for items because they are not paying shipping and they are getting items fast and are dealing with Amazon only, not some sellers they know nothing about.

I like the concept because everyone seems to win. You list the item at any price you want (I try to be just under what other sellers are asking). Aside from inconsequential things like checking out my competition and perhaps reducing prices here and there, Amazon does everything—I mean *everything*—for you once you have listed and mailed the items to one of their warehouses. FBA is Amazon's baby. Sure, there are fees you have to pay, but the amount they charge, in my opinion, does not even come close to outweighing the hassle of having to deal with all that stuff. The price in my opinion is more than fair.

There are really no right or wrong answers as to which of Amazon's formats you decide to use. Check out MFN and FBA, investigate a little further, and read online forums. Check out the fees, and go with what you feel comfortable with. Just make sure you always check rules and regulations and keep up with them, this way you are confident in what you are selling.

As for me, just because I only sell books and CDs via FBA does not mean that's how you should do it. I have a few likes, dislikes, and things I've just simply gotten used to doing. My preferences, however, are not necessarily the right or the wrong ways; they're just what I am comfortable with at my level. You may have other ideas, and that's great! This is your gig, your hobby, and your business.

Let's use an analogy. If you wanted to learn bird-watching, you might read a book about it just like you are reading this one. You may talk to other bird watchers, and perhaps go online to research bird-watching, but you won't do the exact same thing every other bird-watcher does. You won't end up going to the same regions, looking at the same birds, or going out only in the daytime or evening. You are going to go bird-watching in a manner that works best for you. It's the same with how you approach my advice; you can follow it exactly or mold it into your own systems. Either way is fine as long as *you* are comfortable with it.

PayPal

Simply stated, PayPal is a huge time-saver. When you open a PayPal account, you can then easily receive and send money in a matter of seconds. You can also, among other things, obtain a PayPal debit card and use it pretty much like any other card you have tied to a bank account. When I sell on eBay, I only accept payment via PayPal, which is commonly used by Internet users, so your potential buyers won't find your preference for it surprising. After a buyer has won one of your auctions, he or she can pay for the item with a click, and—voilà!—you have the funds in your account. However, not all buyers have access to PayPal accounts, but they don't have to; just about any credit card will do. But whether buyers have PayPal or not will really have nothing to do with you. What's important is that the payments end up in your account. In addition, there are going to be times when buyers are not satisfied with their purchases. I will explain how to handle such dissatisfaction in chapter 10, "Keep the Customer Satisfied," but for now let's assume you opt to refund an unhappy buyer's money. You can do this immediately via PayPal. Just remember the overall convenience you gain through using PayPal. There are fees of course; however, not one of those fees has ever bothered me, but do check out its charges for yourself because you should know how much you pay for its service and why.

By now, you have hopefully successfully dipped your toes in the water; it's time to get in a little deeper and start setting up your office. You may be surprised, even shocked how much you can comfortably fit within a small amount of space!

2
Organizing Your "Office"

Amazon FBA note: If you are only going to be selling on Amazon via FBA, an "office" will really not be necessary

Something to Think about before Continuing with This Chapter

AS DISCUSSED IN "Preliminary Thoughts and Ideas and How to Read This Book" and in chapter 1, you have two ways to approach your new hobby: either you will go out on a few Saturdays and test the waters before setting up your office, or if you are comfortable enough, you will set up shop before proceeding. There is no right or wrong answer; this is a simple decision based on your feelings. Again, I would lean more toward the side of spending a few Saturdays in the field before setting yourself up. Whichever way you decide to proceed is just fine. Just make sure you read chapter 3 very carefully, especially the section "Safety First"!

If you do decide to set up your office first, you can now skip the rest of this section and start up in the next section titled "Now Onto the Rest Of The Chapter."

If you prefer, as stated above, you may want to spend a few Saturdays going to garage sales to ensure you enjoy and are productive in them. The problem that arises from not being fully prepared by having an office set up is that the lack of a system is going to make things a little awkward for you. You may end up coming home from your first couple of Saturday excursions with a carload of neat finds to sell, but you won't have an adequate system in place to handle all of your items properly. Avoid retreating from buying; go for it; build up your stock. We'll deal with the liquidation later. I have set up an extremely simple four-point system for you to get through this transition period.

Here's what we're going to do:

1. Find a place in your home to store your finds for the time being—a corner of the garage, under the bed, or really anywhere that's out of the way. A good idea is to keep the items in boxes; otherwise the clutter is going to make you, your significant other, your family, or even your pets very nervous!

2. Avoid attending any more garage sales for now. That may be difficult, because I'm confident you will be very excited about your recent successes at the previous sales. The problem is that if you keep going to garage sales with no systems in place, you are just going to become overwhelmed. It would be like having a clog in a water pipe that has a regular flow of water trying to barrel through. Eventually, a break will happen, resulting in a royal mess. Let's just attend to the inventory we've got and go from there.

3. Use your allotted time during the week and the Saturday mornings spent at home instead of sailing to list and sell just a few of your finds on the Internet. If you limit it to a few, then you won't need an office set up or systems in place. This will provide multiple benefits. First, you will learn the techniques and systems that will help you get used to the process. Second, you'll put a little cash in your pocket, along with a lot of confidence.

4. Once you have sold some items and feel like you really want to move forward with this (and I think you will), then reread chapter 1. Purchase all of your supplies and continue with this

chapter and proceed to put together an office. You will now be in a position to hit your new venture with passion, zeal, and experience that this does work. You'll be able to continue your Saturday-morning excursions into the exciting world of garage sailing.

Now on to the Rest of the Chapter

During my childhood I had been told a saying that I have come to understand the importance of all too well. That saying was KISS, which is an acronym for "Keep it simple, stupid!" I believe that may have been told to me as a child because I was a bit too detail oriented.

I have done my best to incorporate the KISS concept into my life without giving up some of the positive qualities I was born with. Through lots of trial and error, I have fine-tuned both the qualities of simplicity and details and combined them into a healthier way of living, rather than emphasize one side over the other. What does this all mean to you, and why am I sharing some of my personal idiosyncrasies? The answer is simple: I have been able, from my own life experiences, to inject simplicity with detail and organization in a way that will make your learning and implementation of my systems not only easy but also extremely effective. My approach rings especially true with this chapter on how to organize and systemize a small area. Whether you are working out of the corner of a garage or your own bedroom, my system will work well and require only a limited amount of space; thus, you or the rest of your family won't be overwhelmed.

Picking an Area

Give this issue a lot of thought. You need an area that does not get too much foot traffic. For instance, a corner of the kitchen or family room would probably be the worst place to set up your office. Such places are typically high-traffic areas of homes. They also collect the most noise (from televisions, talking, radio, etc.). This is not to say that your family room won't work. It can. It's just that it will not be as conducive to quiet and concentration as I would like to see. The best area would be an unused office or bedroom. In such places, you can close the door behind you, roll up your sleeves, and get to work.

Unfortunately, few people have that luxury. If you do, stop right here and skip this section but not the chapter. You are one step ahead of everyone else, so skip right now to the next section titled "How Much Room Do I Need." For the rest of you, read below, since I provide an itemized list of normal areas that many households have, and these areas are prioritized from best to worst.

**Habitable part of your garage, basement, or enclosed
patio
Occupied bedroom (preferably master), but with a few
furnishings
Loft
Living room
Family or TV room
Area beside the kitchen**

If you live in a small condo or apartment, you may have no choice other than the living room or bedroom. In this case, you simply have to choose which one affords the most space without getting too much in the way of the rest of the household. If you live in a larger home, you should study the list and choose the location that you and the rest of the members of your household feel will provide the quietest and most comfortable space for your new endeavor.

How Much Room Do I Need?
You have narrowed down where you are going to place your office, but exactly how much room are you really going to need without feeling cramped? That is a relative question with relative answers. In

other words, some people may feel claustrophobic in the same-sized area in which another person would feel quite comfortable.

Your Computer and Desk
If you do not have one already, get a simple desk for your computer as well as for other miscellaneous items, such as tape, pens, a tape measure, hand sanitizer etcetera. To make my system work in a small area, you need to use every square inch. Think of your space like an area on a ship. If you have ever been on a cruise or have served in the navy, you know what I'm talking about: there is no wasted space on a ship. Your berth (or bedroom), for example, puts everything at your disposal. If you stand up, you cannot move around much laterally, but if you turn around in a circle, you see that you have all your essentials at your fingertips. I want you to have that same sensation when you regard your office. Your supplies and items should be not only in front of you but also all around and within reach. Using the corner of any room should make things even more compact for you.

Closet Space
If you have chosen a bedroom in which to put your office, if possible, I want you to place your desk at arm's length to the closet, thus saving valuable space and time. If you plan to work without a closet, put inexpensive plastic shelving against a wall near your desk. Having placed the shelving in the appropriate area, you can now use it for some of your bulkier items that will not fit on your computer desk, such as DVD and CD envelopes. You can store such items for easy accessibility on the first two shelves. You might be surprised to find out how many other items you can fit on four fourteen-inch-deep shelves.

Excess DVDs and CDs
As the months go by, you will find yourself accumulating excess DVDs and CDs—ones that did not sell or were not worth listing. These kinds

of media items have great profit potential by selling in bulk, which we will discuss in more detail in chapter 7. For the time being, however, you need to properly store these items so that they do not hinder your daily routine. I find my having a number of banker-style boxes ready to be highly prudent. As stated earlier, they typically come in packs of ten and end up only costing about a couple of bucks apiece. Each box holds about 175 CDs or about seventy-five DVDs. You can stack these boxes easily in the corner of a room, out of the way of everything else.

Closet Space
If you have chosen a bedroom, all or even just part of the closet is going to help tremendously. You can easily get by using just a small part of the closet, depending on its size. Many closets already have shelving in them. If yours does not, I recommend installing some inexpensive shelving.

Plastic Shelving
As I mentioned in the supplies section of chapter 1 and previously in the closet space section, plastic shelving is a must; it maximizes space and organization. You can purchase it at just about any home improvement outlet or warehouse. It is very inexpensive and a perfect replacement if you have no closet or if the closet you have is already being used.

Wallflowers
Whenever I think of a wallflower, I picture a shy girl or boy standing in a corner and leaning up against a wall at a high school dance. They are painfully self-conscious and hope no one sees them. They simply want to become invisible (or so they think, but we won't get into teenage psychology right now). The point I'm trying to make is that you need to make some of your items invisible or, at the least, turn them into a part of your room.

You can easily do this with just a little imagination. Find an unused corner of your room and get creative. Use twenty-by-twenty-inch boxes that are also twenty inches deep. They conform perfectly to the corners of rooms, and there's no reason why they should retain that ugly brown cardboard color. Why not decorate them with either colorful wrapping paper or wallpaper? Use something that blends well with your decor and taste. You can use these boxes for storing just about anything—from a large envelope full of vintage movie photos, to a collectible fishing reel, or even awkward or unsightly items.

Garage Basements and Enclosed Patios
If you have decided to utilize a space in your garage, basement, or enclosed patio area, just follow the same format above. Just make sure, as with a bedroom, that you try to utilize a corner and that you take advantage of shelving.

If you do your best to adhere to the above instructions, you will find that you can set up your office in a very small space. You will gain not only adequate room to make my systems work but may even have excess room. After cleverly utilizing your chosen space, you will be surprised at how much you can fit into one small area.

My last bit of advice is to get creative. You may find that some of my suggestions don't seem to work well for you. That's okay, but hopefully my ideas spark your imagination. Design an office that works well for you by basing it on your particular needs and sur-roundings. My suggestions are just that, suggestions, so if you find a way that saves even more room and adds comfort to your workplace, implement it!

Storing Surplus Supplies
Once you really get going on this, you will want to buy some of your supplies in bulk. Doing so is less expensive and much less of a hassle than continually having to purchase these things. Items such as tape,

labels, and pens obviously take up very little space, but other supplies, such as boxes, envelopes, and Bubble Wrap may be rather large and awkward. Because these are surplus items, you obviously do not need daily access to them. If you can avoid it, do not keep surplus items in your office, this is where you should utilize space like your attic, garage, or basement. It's best to store them somewhere out of the way that is still somewhat easy to get to, at the very least, on the top shelf of your plastic shelving, as long as the items are not too heavy.

And there you go, the boring stuff is now over; let's move on to the Saturday mornings!

3
Saturday Morning Has Arrived

Time to Set Sail

CHECK THOSE WEATHER reports! Obviously, if it's raining, you won't be going out, but let's take it a step further. If your local weathercaster told everyone there's a high likelihood of rain, but precipitation is not looming overhead, you should still stay home. The reason is that people preparing for garage sales are watching the same weather reports. If there is a decent chance of rain, many, if not most of them avoid setting up for a sale. Let Thursday be the cutoff day for you. If on Thursday the local weathercaster says there is a high chance of rain for Friday or Saturday, that's it; even if the sun is beating down on you on either of those two days, just stay home. If on Thursday your weathercaster says there is little to no chance of rain for Friday or Saturday, and if in fact it does not rain, go for it, happy sailing!

But what if no matter what the report says, it ends up raining on Friday? I'm not talking just a little short-lived drizzle but rather a somewhat rainy day? The answer is that it's best to just stay home even if it's clear on Saturday. The reason is because many persons holding the garage sale use Friday to prepare; in addition if it's raining on Friday, they may be concerned it will continue into Saturday. The only other exception would be fog. If you wake up on Saturday morning to a layer of fog, staying indoors is a smart bet, at least until it lifts, if for no other reason than safety.

To prepare yourself for sailing, you need to begin on Friday; you want to start your route on Saturday fully prepared. Make sure you have a full tank of gas and at least $150 in cash. This amount will increase as you become more experienced and start making money. It is important that you have about $50 in small bills; $5 and $1 bills are preferred. I can almost guarantee that if you do not have small bills, you will come across a winner item for a buck, and it will be too early in the morning for the seller to have change. I preach from experience! Also, have some loose change, mostly quarters. To be honest even if something is a dime, I'll still hand them a quarter and tell them to not worry about it; fifteen cents is a cheap price to spread a little goodwill!

So now the weather reports are positive, and you have a full tank of gas and cash in your pocket. You're ready to go. Keep a cardboard box or preferably a plastic container in your back seat and/or trunk, and you can put your various finds in it. To buy a small cooler would be a good investment. You can purchase the ones about the size of a lunchbox for right around ten bucks. Throw in some bottled water, fruit, an energy bar, or whatever you're so inclined to munch on. If you bring a cooler, you can pull over somewhere and reenergize yourself without taking valuable time away from your objective with things like having to go into a grocery store or waiting in a long line at a fast-food place.

Saturday is the only time when you cannot pick and choose when you want to work at garage sailing. Every single minute is important, because each minute could mean finding those items that will make all your efforts pay off. You will hear this stated a few times: it's a numbers game. I remember when I first started, there was one Saturday when I was so discouraged that I felt I may as well just go home and watch some television. The pickings were dry out there. There were lots of garage sales but very little in the way of good items. This situation shouldn't happen often, but it will happen. I stuck with it, and literally at the very last sale I attended—bam!—I found one item that made me over $1,000. I can assure you I was glad I didn't go home and lay on my couch watching TV.

Rise and Shine

The time at which you set your alarm should depend on how long it takes you to get ready. Just make sure you are up and out the door so you are at the beginning of your route between seven and seven thirty in the morning.

You may have heard that some people start even earlier than this. Although that's true, I don't like it, and here's why: you may be up and raring to go at, say, six in the morning, but some sellers may be just getting up. The few times I have started a little earlier, I've noticed some sellers were just putting up their signs. If you miss the signs, you miss the sales. Even if you see signs, they may have been placed there the night before meaning your destination may not be open yet. Also, if it's early in the morning, some sellers may still be in the process of putting out their merchandise. The last thing you want to do at six in the morning is stand in someone's front yard waiting for him or her to put out the goods. In the world of garage sales, you would be referred to as being an "early bird" in this situation. And guess what? People holding garage sales are not crazy about early birds! I feel starting your route no earlier than 7:00 a.m. or 7:30 a.m. and no later than 8:00 a.m. is a good window of time to follow. That said, experiment a little on your particular area; see if starting early would be more beneficial to you.

I've found that by around seven or so in the morning, a decent percentage of the signs are up and by eight even more. So even if you start at eight, you're still going to be okay. If you're eager and still want to start early, then here's what you do: go for it, but have a route before your regular route. In other words, plan to go to an area that is not on your normal route. Drive it, and get in as many sales as you can. Just make sure you end up at the beginning of your real route at around seven thirty give or take. This may also work to your benefit if for some reason you have to quit sailing early. My advice is to get in about six hours on Saturday. I have found that approximately seven thirty to around one thirty, maybe two in the afternoon at the latest works best and is the most productive time frame for me. After around twelve thirty to one, lots of people start wrapping up, resulting in fewer sales. Fewer sales equates to fewer chances of finding resalable items. Use your time wisely.

Your Competition
You will find that the first hour or so of sailing is the busiest. After about eight or nine in the morning, you should notice that the sales are much less crowded; in some cases, you may be the only one there. Does this mean all the good deals are gone? Not in the least! Keep in mind that there might not be as many so-called professionals out there as you think. And anyway they cannot be at every sale at the same time. Sure, there will be some really cool deals made early, but I have to tell you that I've found some awesome items very far into the day. Now if there were a lot of professionals out there, don't you think they would have nabbed those prizes I found?

I never give so-called professionals a second thought. Admittedly, I used to think that if I missed the rush during the early hours of the morning, I might as well just go home, crawl back in bed, and throw a blanket over my head. How wrong I was! To prove this to myself, I forced myself to stick with it, good or bad, until about one or two in the afternoon. I did this for my first few Saturdays. What I discovered was that there were probably few, if any professionals out there!

Bear in mind that my systems are geared toward making as much profit in the shortest time possible. You do not have to be an antique dealer to make this work, as you will learn in chapter 5, "Antiques, Vintage Stuff, and Collectibles—How to Recognize Value." As a matter of fact, I am absolutely amazed at how many good deals are left behind even after hordes of people have rummaged through the sales. Ignore the crowds and the few professionals *that might* be out there. As a matter of fact, here's a curious thought that may change the way you feel: after a few months, in a sense *you* will be the professional! If you stick with this, you will learn more and more each Saturday, and even on your downtime as you research things. You will be like a sponge soaking up loads of information on the process as well as learning the skill of recognizing salable items. I am still learning and constantly discovering something new that helps me spot value items.

Follow the Signs

As you are driving your route, you will see signs advertising a garage, yard, or estate sale. Avoid concerning yourself too much with the address since a seller typically does a pretty good job steering pass-ersby to his or her home by using arrows. My favorite sign makers are those who use large, bright-yellow poster boards with bold black ink.

Strangely, I've found an interesting phenomenon when it comes to signs. If it is large and bright, as I have stated, chances are the sale will also be large with lots of fun stuff to go through. If, on the other hand, the sign is small and looks to be written with a ballpoint pen, chances are you may have a loser sale on your hands. This is unfortu-nately not a hard-and-fast rule, so go ahead and attend all the sales, big signs or not. If, however, for some reason you are on a tight sched-ule and think you cannot complete your route, then consider avoiding following these weak signs to free up your time for healthier ones.

There are those people out there who will post signs on telephone poles or whatever extremity is available, signs that simply state "Garage or Yard Sale" and the pertinent addresses but no arrows. These signs don't do much good if there are no arrows pointing the way for potential customers. Unless you happen to live in that par-ticular neighborhood, you are never going to find the addresses of these sales. Don't even try. Certainly do not waste your time looking up the addresses on your smartphone or car navigator. This is unnec-essary, since garage sales are generally abundant on Saturdays. Just skip such sales, and go to the next ones. You're better off utilizing your time properly than aimlessly searching for a sale with no arrows to point you in the right direction.

Undoubtedly, the time will come where you find yourself follow-ing a sign with arrows that lead to nothing. Talk about frustration, especially if such arrows lead you down a long path. I remember one sunny Saturday when things were going very well. I was hitting lots of sales and making good deals. I had a nice, steady pace going. I saw this sign that led to a kind of rural area adjacent to a more concentrated group of homes.

I thought, Hey, I bet there's a great sale there...perhaps older, larger, and expensive properties...probably a huge opportunity.

I gave into temptation and followed the signs, and every time I was about to give up, another one would pop up around the corner. I kept following...and following...and following up a very windy road. Before I knew it, I was way off my route and severely frustrated. I never did find the sale. The worst was that I was lost and did not know my way back. It took me more than a half hour just to find my route. I could have hit a number of sales during that time period. More than likely, these signs were from the previous week or two, or maybe they just quit early but didn't think to take their signs down out of consideration for the attendees! Leaving a sign up is, quite frankly, rude and irresponsible. The situation does happen and more so towards the end of the day. People quit but still leave their signs up, this may cause you to feel a bit of irritation. Let it bounce right off you. Never forget that this is all about having fun and, yes, making money, of course. For the most part, however, I have found sellers to be both responsible and intelligent when it comes to sign making.

There is a way that helps avoid this situation. If you see a sign that seems faded, looks a little worn, or is curling on the sides, chances are that it had been up there awhile. Just skip it, as it is probably a phantom sale. Do not feel as though you need to follow every sign and attend every single sale. There are also going to be times when you're following legitimate signs, but your doing so takes you farther and farther out of your way just like in the previous example. Again, you must ask yourself if that sale is worth the time you are taking to find it. Chasing sales is usually a mistake. Look at it this way: for every out- of-area sale you skip, you are raising your odds of fitting in a few that might be chock-full of opportunity.

Keep On Going

Okay, you see a sign in all its glory. It's new, it's bright, and it has arrows leading the way. Bravo! It leads you to a legitimate garage sale. Now you have to make the decision whether you even want to get out of your car. I have found a way to tell if a sale is going to be a flop: look for lots and lots of clothes strewn upon the front lawn, which makes the sale appear bigger than it actually is, or there is only a handful of items, and you can see clearly from your car that it is nothing you are interested in. You may also note whether there are what looks to be only furniture or other large items. In situations like these, you have to make a judgment call. There is always the possibility that if you get out of your car and start walking closer to the sale, you will find knickknacks in boxes that you could not see from the street; again, it's a judgment call.

Sometimes sales are obvious losers, and in other cases, you're really never going to know for sure until you inspect them. Make the best decision you can and go with it; try not to second-guess yourself. Once again, it is a—you guessed it—numbers game. I probably skip about a dozen or more of these types of sales in a day, which frees up my time, allowing me to go to other profit-rich garage sales. I have one footnote, though: park your car on the side of the street and then look at the sale. Safety first—do not slow down your speed and strain to see what kind of items are in people's yards. An unsafe move like that is simply not worth the various problems that can result. On that same note, as you pull up to a garage sale, try to be considerate of anyone who may be pulling up behind you; even if there is no one there, there probably will be very soon. If appropriate pull up as far as you can to give them room to park their car.

Estate Sales

Let me say just one thing before we move on—professionals! I have rarely gone to an estate sale and found anything of value that was priced so attractively that I felt I could make a decent profit. It was not for a lack of effort. I remember one instance for example. I went to an estate sale late in the day and found a table loaded with old cameras.

Wow, I thought, there's got to be great value here.

They were asking something like twenty-five dollars per camera (this should have been my first clue to run, which I will discuss more in chapter 4, "Negotiations"). They said if I bought them all, I could have them for fifteen dollars apiece. How could I refuse? Yours truly just knew one or more of these cameras had to be a rare find worth many times than what they were asking for since the cameras looked so old. As it turned out, I was lucky to sell my "rare" find for about half of what I paid.

I can hear planners of estate sales scoffing at me and my remarks, so let me rephrase and clarify myself. I have rarely (yes, there are exceptions) gone to an estate sale and found anything of value that could be resold on the Internet for a worthwhile profit. Professional estate sales are planned and executed by people who understand value, who know or have already researched the Internet demand for certain things, and who do this for a living. These sales will more than likely be devoid of the kind of items that make my systems work. Buying at an estate sale would be like getting on the Internet, buying an item from a seller who is familiar with antiques, vintage stuff, and collectibles, and then reselling it online for a profit. Sure, you might get lucky, but the odds, in my opinion, are so low that you are better off putting your energies and money elsewhere.

Every rule seems to have its own exceptions, however. In regard to estate sales, let me share four reasons, or exceptions why you should stop at them.

Buying for yourself

Yes, you might find something for yourself or someone else—an item that you really want to buy and do not mind paying estate-sale prices for. Remember, estate-sale pricing can still be good; it's just that in general they don't leave enough meat on the bone so to speak for you to make a decent profit. Finding cool things for yourself at an estate sale is just one of the many perks of sailing. I don't mind paying estate-sale prices for something I really want or something I collect. I can still get a decent deal, only not at garage-sale prices. That's okay because the item is for me personally and not for resale. Evaluate some of the things you like. Do you collect anything in particular? If not, should you start a collection? I am of the firm belief that collecting items from some sort of genre you have an affinity for is healthy. Collections are enjoyable to look at and to display your dedication and effort, and they can be very good investments. Just avoid attending estate sales thinking you are going to make a tidy profit; odds are you will not.

Your Own Expertise
The second reason to attend an estate sale is that you believe you are more of an expert in some area than the estate-sale planner. Hey, they can't know everything! Let's say you know quite a bit about a certain time period of décor and furniture. You now have a larger advantage than does anyone else, quite possibly including the estate-sale planner.

Is It a Professional Estate Sale?
The third reason it's worth stopping at estate sales is if the sign leading to it is written in magic marker or for whatever reason just does not look very professional. If that's the case, go for it! In this instance, there is a chance the proprietor has no idea what an estate sale means. He or she is just using the word because it sounds cool or maybe thinks it will attract more people. It might actually be an estate sale, but it might not be a professionally handled one. Perhaps a relative of the seller has passed away, and he or she is selling the entire estate. In this case, give it a shot.

DVDs, CDs, and Books
The fourth exception is to buy DVDs, CDs, and books. If for no other reason, stop at any estate sale for these items. Chances are that the

people whose estates are being liquidated were older and that they either passed, moved in with family, or went into some kind of senior or assisted living. Many older people are avid readers; you may come across some great book finds. I once came across a handful of books all about wood working that I bought for a few bucks and resold for a handsome profit, and that *was* at an estate sale, so this can happen. Elderly people also may have older DVDs and CDs. These are some of the best online sellers. You are not going to find Britney Spears or Justin Bieber CDs, but you may find artists like Burt Bacharach or Doris Day. The older stuff like that is typically not that abundant, so such items can have a huge potential value. It is the same with DVDs. I find a lot of BBC (British Broadcasting Company) released series at estate sales. These are not easy to find, but a lot of elderly people enjoy and collect a more highbrow selection of movies—lots of value in that type of genre.

The Estate-Sale Planner

If you happen to be in the estate-sale business and you are reading this book, please try not to take offense from what I have said and what I am about to say. That stated, some estate-sale planners (note I said some) can seem to be in a bit of a bad mood and do not act like they much enjoy what they are doing; this is not necessarily true. Keep in mind this is not entirely fun for them. They do this for a living, and they take it very seriously, as they should. In a sense you are coming to their place of employment. Planning and executing an estate sale is an awful lot of work and is not a one day thing; rather it can take weeks or more to put together a professional estate sale. They have a huge amount of things going on all in the short span of a few hours, and remember that the family who have hired them are depending on them to do an excellent job, which means the estate planner has an awful lot of responsibility. So take this into consideration if you feel a bit of perceived negativity coming your way.

This is one of the reasons I advised you to zero in on the reasons or exceptions why you should go to an estate sale and try to avoid viewing it like a normal garage sale. If, however, you choose to move forward trying to make a deal for resale purposes, try to make them a somewhat reasonable offer and preferably later in the day; otherwise if you get shot down, you may end up taking it too personally. The planners can be very abrupt at times. I find for myself I rarely try to make a deal because I'd have to get the item so much lower than what they are asking for; that it's really not worth my energy. Impossible? No, you may for whatever reason get a smoking deal, but it's my opinion to always try to keep the odds and the positive vibes in our favor. Uncomfortable situations such as abruptness can certainly take the wind off your sails.

That said, I will almost always try to make a deal on buying a collection of DVDs, CDs, or books, often all three at one time. It's not like you're buying a one-hundred-year-old grandfather clock that the family is very attached to. Things such as DVDs, CDs, and books can sometimes be looked at more as inconsequential items. Later in the day especially, they may be open to making you a lucrative deal to take a bunch if not all of these off their hands. It's worth a try. On that same note, try to get a feel for who's in charge; the people they have working for them might not have the authority to make a deal.

One final word: you may very well end up over time recognizing the estate-sale planner from previous sales, so be pleasant, and if they're not real busy, start a little small talk, not so much about what they're selling but rather *anything* else, or perhaps compliment them on their expertise to understand value. It will be a refreshing change for them, and they'll probably remember you in a nice way, which is always a good thing whenever you are on the other side of a negotiation!

Rummage Sales
These will typically be for some kind of charity, or often held by a church. I love them, especially later in the day. The volunteers want the relevant stuff gone, or the items are probably going to a donations center. You are doing them a favor by getting as much of the

stuff off their hands as possible. Plus, there is no personal attachment to items at rummage sales and no rhyme or reason as to what
you may find there since they came from multiple donors.

Block Sales

Block sales are usually not for charity. They're often an annual thing
that some neighborhoods do to get rid of unwanted items. The problem is that since the sellers often conduct these sales every year,
there's not that much good stuff like things that came from the
closet, attic, or garage rafters. I still stop, park, and walk as fast as
possible from one sale to the next. I rarely score big, but I can fit in a
large number of sales in a very short period of time without driving
around, so the potential lack of resalable items somewhat balances
with my ability to hit multiple sales. Also, keep in mind these neighbors have been talking about their stuff for days or even weeks, and
often one of the neighbors will pick up a treasure before anyone else.
That neighbor knew about the particular item before the signs even
went up! But don't pass up on block sales, for no other reason than to
pick up more DVDs, CDs, and books.

As in anything that might be unfamiliar to you, garage sailing
may take a little time to get used to. However, with any new learning
experience, the more you do it, the easier, faster, and more efficient
you become at it. The same holds true for sailing. All the things you
do during the week to make your new hobby a success can be done at
your leisure with no set hours or time limit. But this is not true with
the actual sailing part. The more quality sales you hit the more successful you will be.

Thrift Stores

This book is about buying at garage, yard, and estate sales only; however, I know a lot of you will be wondering or have been told that thrift
stores are a great profit potential. Although this can be true, there
are some things I would like to address regarding thrift stores. Many
of the proprietors have become very savvy with regard to value; they

have access to the same information we all do and quite often are not going to let a treasure escape them. Thrift stores can sell online too and often do. In addition they sometimes can be open seven days a week unlike garage sales that are a one time shot and only have a six hour or so window. Buyers can go to thrift stores at their leisure, not so with garage sales. In other words there's much more competition at thrift stores.

Can you make a profit buying at thrift stores? Of course you can, but I feel that you are better off putting the odds in your favor. That said, if you are so inclined, drop in every now and then. You can even make it a regular thing if you have the time during the week or even on Saturdays when because of the weather or time of the year it's not yielding garage sales. You will be basically doing the same thing I am teaching you in this book with regard to spotting value. I would say you are better off going to the smaller independent thrift stores rather than the larger chains.

There is one exception, always an exception, right! If you have a niche, thrift stores could be a very good revenue for you. For instance I knew someone who did nothing but buy clothes at thrift stores and resell on Amazon. They actually did it full time and made a living out of it, not huge but a regular income all the same. There is nothing to say that this person could not have expanded on their business and in a big way; they just seemed comfortable at that particular time with their level, which is okay, but rest assured the potential to expand is there as would be with any specialization.

Every now and then I will stick my head in a thrift store, and yes, I've found a few things here and there that I have made a profit with, but again, it is my opinion that you are not putting the odds fully in your favor buying at thrift stores as opposed to garage sales.

You may have heard about book buyers buying at thrift stores and selling on Amazon. It's true. I've found a few salable books myself, but I have found that for the most part thrift stores ask too much for books. Some buyers use an app on their smartphone to quickly scan books to see if they are worth buying. I don't have the patience or the desire to do this; however, it could be something you might be interested in doing. There is no right or wrong answer. There are other books on the market that deal with thrift stores and their potential profit. If it's something you are interested in, you should look into it. Now let's get back to what this particular book is all about: garage, yard, and estate sales!

Remember Where You Are!
Very often I would leave my car, get out to the sale, and be there a while. Perhaps I got caught up in the excitement of a great find or perhaps even got involved in some friendly conversation. By the time I got back to my car, I had no idea in which direction I entered onto the street! It's a very unsettling feeling and can also waste a lot of time. Just try to be cognizant of where you are when you arrived and in which direction you need to go to get back on your route.

Safety First
Now comes the lecture part of this book. Do *not* skip this! Just as you learned when you were a kid in school, "Safety always comes first." This is also true with sailing. No matter what you venture into, you will find safety rules. No one can avoid them. If you decided to take up bike riding, you'd have rules to follow. Photography has rules. Golf? Trust me, lots of rules! Knitting? Believe it or not, knitting has rules; for instance, you wouldn't want to leave one of those knitting needles around when there's a child in the house. Every hobby has a unique set of rules, and so does sailing. Here are some rules that will hopefully keep you and innocent bystanders out of trouble.

Drive Safely
As you are on your mission to find garage sales, remember that you are driving a car! If for example you are driving down a road and a garage sale sign suddenly pops out at you that does not mean you can immediately brake! Just be careful; drive safely and defensively as you are looking for sales and signs.

People!

Slow down! Is it that important you get there a nanosecond earlier than the guy in front of you? Of course it isn't. You should always drive safely but in reference to garage sales, keep in mind it is Saturday, and with that come a few red flags. Earlier in the day, some people may not be quite awake yet, even though they are out and about. Maybe they had a wild Friday night; maybe they're just tired from the previous week, or perhaps they're just not morning people. Be conscious of this and keep in mind it works both ways. You also need to be careful of inept drivers as you are walking to and from a garage sale.

Kids!

You should be equally careful seven days a week, but remember on Saturdays school is usually out. Kids are going to be running all over the place, maybe some from the garage sale or perhaps others neighborhood kids; whatever the case rest assured there will be kids out there, so *be careful*! You are driving through residential neighborhoods on a weekend. This is a time when there is usually less traffic and more kids playing in the streets. And those kids might not be expecting more traffic than normal.

Elderly People

Be aware of elderly people, at the sales, walking, driving in their cars, etcetera. Also sometimes a seniors-only group of homes or perhaps a seniors-only mobile home park will have a sort of "block" sale. Just be aware of your surroundings.

Too Much Happening at One Time

When arriving at a garage sale, really slow down and concentrate on safety. There is *a lot* going on. For instance some (actually quite a few!) people don't stop and pull over but rather just slow down to look at garage sales, doing exactly what I told you not to do earlier. I see it all the time; so will you. They look at their potential new couches or other items, not the people and cars around them. They do what I taught you to do: they check out the sales before taking the time to get out of their cars. But they didn't read my book; they're checking out sales while driving! Just be careful, and use your common sense. Drive safely and defensively, and you won't regret it.

Questionable Areas

There are also times when you see a sign for a garage sale, but it is leading you to an area that you are just not comfortable with. Skip it! Use your common sense. It's just not worth it.

Apartments

Sometimes you will see garage sales held in someone's apartment. Yes, apartment complexes may have garage sales too. They are often held right in the apartment itself, since there may not be a garage or yard. The same could be said for a sale being held in someone's home. Is it worth the risk? Only if for whatever reason you feel very confident and comfortable with the situation.

Alleys

Occasionally, you are going to be led to a sale that requires you to drive down a back alley. Now there are some neighborhoods, I would say probably more of the older ones, that have alleys where the garages are generally detached and in the back; in these cases, the alley is like a road, although generally a narrow one. If the alley is relatively open and you feel okay, go for it; otherwise, again, just use your best judgment. Take heed of what your parents taught you growing up: better safe than sorry. Listen to that little voice in your head—it's usually right!

Watch your step

Your eyes might be fixed on all the cool stuff you're about to look at. Just be careful, watch your step, there may be things like a sprinkler in a yard or crack in the driveway you do not notice, aside from the potential physical danger it's VERY embarrassing taking a fall in someone's yard with people all around you!

Watch Your Money

Avoid flashing cash; try to be discrete with your money when pay-ing the seller. Do not have anything larger than a twenty-dollar bill. When you are handing the money over always announce how much you are giving them, not in an obnoxious way rather just loud enough so you know they can here you. If, for example you just purchased an item for eight dollars and you are giving them a twenty then simply say it out loud "Here's a twenty-dollar bill." It's not really a matter of trust; rather I am concerned that with all the confusion of run-ning a garage sale, they may forget what you gave them and perhaps thought it was a ten-dollar bill or less; now you are in a very awkward position. I speak from experience; I had this happen and simply chose to leave without my money, but I can assure you, it never happened again. Always try to learn from your mistakes; your systems will get tighter and your profits higher.

Lock Your doors

You have a lot of stuff in your car, hopefully some very valuable things! Why tempt fate? Just do a quick door lock and you won't have to worry about anything. However I will tell you for years I did not lock my doors and I never had a problem but again…why tempt fate?

Many of the hints in this chapter I am giving you come from simple common sense, but we all, myself included, sometimes forget about common sense in the excitement of the venture. Use your common sense in all aspects of safety not just what I mentioned above. I was very motivated to make garage sailing work. I knew the only way I could make money, have fun, be safe, and do it all in a short period of time would be to develop rules and to stick with them. I strongly urge you to learn from me and my trial and error. After reading this book, you will be able to avoid spending countless hours making the same mistakes I did!

4
Negotiations

Are You a Salesperson?

I'VE OFTEN HEARD people say, "That one is a natural-born salesperson!"

True, some people have that certain something about them that makes people trust and listen to them. This, of course, is a perfect recipe for enabling one person to persuade another to make some kind of decision. But is that a natural-born talent? To a degree, perhaps it is, but I believe that every single one of us has the ability to persuade another person to do something. We all possess that certain something commonly known as charisma, and we all use it every day, without even knowing it.

A shy, introverted person who might feel too self-conscious asking if he or she can get a dollar off a purchase at a garage sale could still ask or accept going on a date. That is essentially a sales job. Furthermore, that person can get hired for a job, which tells me that he or she has successfully persuaded another person to give him or her money for a service. That is certainly a sales job. How about buying a car? The person selling it is not necessarily the only salesperson in the transaction; it can take two!

I don't want to belabor the point; I just want to make it obvious that we all—every single one of us—have an internal ability to sell.

It may, however, be dormant. The good news is that you can easily awaken it.

Some people do have a bit more of a natural gift to sell, and these people often nurture the skill and make a living using it. If you are one of these people, then great. But if you are not, you will only need to nurture a very small amount of it for the sake of sailing. Keep in mind that you are only buying low-priced items at garage sales. You need just enough salesmanship to help you purchase typically used items at even better prices than what they are being offered at. A dollar saved here and there will add up faster than you might think.

Look at it this way: Let's say you go out on a Saturday and find $200 worth of good deals and you are willing to pay the asking price. Using some simple negotiating strategies however, you manage to save an average of 25–50 percent or more off that asking price (doing so is very easy and is expected in most cases). If that's the case, each Saturday you could effectively save anywhere from $50 to $100, which would be approximately $200 to $400 per month, or you might end up saving much more. What's more, negotiating is fun— not just for you but for many of the sellers. Keep in mind that most garage sales are held by people just like you. Most sellers are simply trying to get rid of stuff to make a little extra cash and have some fun all at the same time. They're typically not professionals or fast-talking salespeople, but they do understand the game of the buyer trying to get an even better deal and will usually respond well to it.

Many times I've witnessed a situation at a garage sale in which a buyer asks a seller the price of an item. The seller responds, and the buyer accepts. If you witness such interactions, you will often see a slight expression of surprise on the proprietors' faces; most sellers expect and are ready for buyers to make offers. This is a normal course of events in the world of garage sales. In this chapter, you will come to learn some very simple and basic techniques that will enable you to save money, be amiable, and make negotiating fun for both you and the seller.

Spotting Professional Holding the Garage Sale

Before you learn to spot a professional, you must first understand what a professional is. The answer is literally in the word itself: *professional*. In other words, a professional is someone performing something as a *profession*. In the context of garage sales, professionals are typically people who negotiate the sales of lower-end items on a regular basis. For the most part, you should skip the garage sales that professionals hold. You can often discern one of these sales just by driving by; if not, you will when you walk onto the front yard. Here is how you do both.

Repeat Sales

The most obvious sign is that you saw the same sale last week and perhaps the week before. Typically, repeat sales do not occur because the seller has a lot of stuff to sell; rather, the seller holds garage sales on a regular basis. Most sellers do one garage sale, sell what they can, and then give the rest to charity—simple as that. Professionals are different. They will try to milk every penny out of every item. If certain things don't sell in one day, the professionals believe those items will probably sell at another time. That firm belief is not a good attitude in which to negotiate with.

The Sign

The garage-sale sign may be very professional looking. It does not look like a homemade sign; rather, it is uncharacteristically large and has an "I'm in business" look to it. Or a particular sign could be written on wood or metal, implying the seller uses the sign over and over again.

New Items

You may see lots of new items at such sales, as if they are stores. These types of sellers may purchase their inventories at low costs, intending to sell them on Saturdays. You are thus unlikely to find resalable items as they are *already* being resold.

The Same Items
You may observe a common denominator among the items for sale. If you see a general theme, you should consider that you might have just walked into a sort of outside Saturday store. Keep walking. Let's say you see that a particular sale has everything related to sports, so you realize the seller is a sports enthusiast. All this seller wants to do is sell sports stuff; doing so is their thing, perhaps even a business. This obvious passion, however, is a huge neon sign advertising the presence of a professional, because people generally become experts on what they are passionate about.

Fast Refusals
You may find that when you do make offers to professionals, they flatly refuse without even trying to bargain. It is obvious that these types of sellers are not very motivated. True, occasionally average sellers can be difficult, but it's the professionals who are the typically standoffish negotiators.

Higher-than-Normal Prices
The price quoted or marked on professionals' items may be higher than you would expect. If this is the case, chances are the proprietor has already researched the items and priced them at or just below what they're worth. Does this mean it is definitely a poor deal? No, not at all. You may get lucky and buy an item that is worth much more, but you do not put the odds in your favor when you purchase items at what seems to be deliberately set prices. The only exception should occur if you have personal knowledge that a particular item is a good deal or if that little voice inside your head (or your trusty smartphone) is telling you to buy it.

Small Talk
You may overhear sellers talking about eBay or what have you, or they may converse about antiques and collectibles in general. These are usually people who have done their research and want top dollar.

This, however, is not true every time, which is why you have to listen to the context of what they're talking about when they bring up Internet sales. You must understand that *you* have an online system in place, unlike most people. Selling something on the Internet is generally not the kind of thing someone does just once. Opening an account and going through the whole process just to sell an item or two is a waste of time, not to mention frustrating for most people. In general, people would rather sell items for less at garage sales than deal with setting up online accounts to sell those items. So try to read between the lines in their discourse. Their impatience could be your gain!

Well Preserved

Some of the more collectible items may be well preserved in some way, such as being wrapped in plastic. Typically, only professionals have the desire or know-how to preserve their items. An old stack of comic books, for example, just sitting in a dusty box may be worth a mint. But what if each comic in that same stack is safely wrapped in a plastic magazine bag? Forget about buying them, you are probably dealing with a professional.

Of course, every rule has an exception. Situations may present themselves when someone, not a professional, is selling items from the estate of another person who has passed on, moved away, or gone into retirement. Now this is different than estate sales, which I talk about in chapter 3. I am making reference to someone who is holding an everyday garage sale with stuff his or her friend or family member left behind. Now, there are times when that absent person was a collector or professional and took care of his or her collection by protecting it from the elements like in my example of the comic books. I once purchased a collection of twenty or so vintage golf clubs from a gentleman who was selling all of his (probably deceased) grandfather's items. The clubs were wrapped in plastic, and they were each personally autographed by golf professionals, some very well known! He had no use for them and just wanted someone to take these cumbersome objects off his hands and for a very good price. This is a good example of a situation where you can pick up collectible items in well-maintained conditions at garage-sale prices. The grandfather in this case was the collector or professional not the grandson who had zero desire to be either a collector or a professional in golf memorabilia. Such situations do not happen often, but rest assured they do happen.

Does this mean you should skip all professional sales? Aside from the rare exception, for the most part yes. They hurt time management. The odds of you finding great deals can be slim. The only time I would make an exception to this rule is if I were trying to find something for myself. In cases like this, it's okay to spend more money than the norm because you are not buying for resale. Just don't spend too much time doing this. Remember that on Saturdays, time is money.

To Deal or Not to Deal
And that's a great question! I have outlined a few scenarios that should help you realize when it's appropriate to wheel and deal, when it's wise to walk away, and when it's time to just pay a seller's price and run.

An Obviously Great or Even a Good Deal
You will find yourself in situations where you come across items that are such great deals that it would not benefit you to barter with the sellers—if anything, negotiating could hurt you. You don't want to tempt fate or give someone else the chance to outbid you. Just pay the asking price and get the heck out of that sale as fast as possible.

This has happened to me more than a few times. I'll be at a sale and see what is obviously a fantastic find. The temptation is to barter and get a better deal, but I try to avoid that. Although it's probably just in my mind, I feel as though other garage sale attendees are watching me out of the corner of their eyes, just waiting for me to underbid the item so they can swoop in and get the catch of the day.

Why take that chance? Saving a few dollars is just not worth it if you already know or have a strong suspicion that you made a great find. The only exception would be if no one else were at the sale. If that's the case make an offer or, quickly ask the seller if he or she would be willing to sell the item at a lower price. If the answer is yes, that's great—you save a few bucks. If the answer is no, nod okay, and buy the item anyway. On this same note, you never want to look too anxious. If you see what you know to be an absolutely great deal, just relax and calmly ask the seller what the asking price is. Also listen for their tone of voice; if the seller has reason to believe that he or she is indeed giving you an extremely good deal, then you may offend the seller by offering less.

How Low Do You Go?
The only other situations in which I don't squabble about a price is if something is priced real low already or if I'm only buying one or two items. Let's say I find a book or two that I think may be worth something. The seller is asking one dollar apiece for them, and they are the only books I'm going to buy. I just give the seller the two bucks and leave it at that. On the other hand, if I am buying ten of those books, I would probably offer five dollars for all. And a bulk purchase can be an assortment of different items. I might have a number of unrelated objects in my hands, so I generally offer one price for the whole lot, a sort of buying-in-quantity deal, or some may refer to it as bundling; most sellers agree to it. Often I don't even have to make the offer; they see all the stuff I have in my hands or in a box and just throw out a price as they really don't want to take the time to go through it all; if it's a fair price, just accept it. To be honest, often the price they give me is lower than what I would have offered!

I'll Take Them All
Let's say I am buying a huge lot of the same item—for example, CDs. If a seller has a box of one hundred CDs and is asking a buck apiece, I would probably offer twenty dollars for the whole lot.

If you do buy an entire lot or box full of the same items, say something like this: "Hi, if I buy all of these, can I give you twenty dollars? I'll just take them off your hands and go through them later." (Please note I did not harshly throw a price at the seller; rather, I politely asked him or her permission if I can get them for this price. Sometimes the asking permission verbiage works and sometimes just nicely throwing out a price works; you will begin over time to know when to use certain phrases and articulations, but rest assured harshness or rudeness is almost always a deal breaker.)

Sometimes immediately or sometimes after some back and forth, the seller ends up almost always agreeing to make a deal. If he or she does not, have a top amount you are willing to pay. For that box of CDs, as an example, if there are not a bunch of common stuff such as teenage pop music CDs in the box, I'd probably go to forty bucks or so. What such offers do is remind sellers why they're having garage sales to begin with: to make a little money and to get rid of stuff they no longer want or need. Sometimes they just need someone like you or me to reiterate that for them.

When I say I'll go through the CDs later, I'm essentially telling sellers that there might be garbage in their collections and that I'll have to accept the risk. The comment also tells them that I'm not going to plop down on their front lawn, have a stretch, and start going through each and every item. They really don't want you to do that, and could you blame them? I've seen buyers do this very thing, and it irritates everyone, including me. Often I want to buy the whole box, but out of courtesy, I really can't negotiate until this person finishes his or her new little project. But then, I just take a breath, relax, smile, and remind myself why I'm there in the first place.

At any rate, with respect to the one hundred CDs (and keep in mind this is just an example; you can use this method with just about anything you buy), I always start by opening up the cases and begin inspecting the discs; my doing so worries them a bit because they begin to wonder whether I might find something bad and change my mind altogether. So they often just agree immediately to my offered payment or make me a very fair counter offer. What's more, this approach is more successful later in the day.

After you offer a price to a seller, start counting the items as if the seller has already said yes. This is what a professional salesperson would call an assumptive close. With this behavior, you imply that your deal is obviously great and that they would be fools to say no. Sometimes the "I'll buy it all" play does not work. Again, take the CDs, for example. If the seller said no, I would perhaps offer to buy all one hundred of the CDs for twenty-five cents each. Hey, that's only five dollars more than what I already offered them. Sometimes sellers just respond better to such offers.

They're Asking Too Much
Some sellers have inflated ideas of the values of their items—so inflated that negotiating might be a futile use of your energy. For example, if a seller is asking three dollars for items you might offer fifty cents or so for, then why even try to negotiate? You would have to get them to sell for one dollar each just to make the deal worth *considering*. Generally I walk away in situations like this, you just have to get a vibe as to whether it's worth a go or not. Another scenario may involve an older antique or collectible item. If you thought twenty-five dollars would be an acceptable amount to spend, and if the seller was asking for one hundred dollars, chances are the seller won't come down to twenty-five dollars. Most likely, I would simply walk away.

But here we go again with another exception! I recall one sale that had a very old antique ice-cream maker. I knew I could probably get seventy-five to one hundred dollars or more for this type of antique. The seller was asking for seventy-five dollars. Normally, I just walk away from such high prices, but at that time, it was already late in the day. From the corner of my eye, I could see the seller just staring at me after she had quoted the price. I had a strong suspicion she really wanted to get rid of this rather clumsy object, so as I was beginning to walk away I turned, looked at the seller, gave a nice smile, and kindly said, "Ten bucks?" The seller immediately agreed. I ended up making a tidy profit of about one hundred dollars.

Remember that the vast majority of sellers' number-one objective for garage sales is to get rid of as much stuff as possible and as fast as possible while still making some money. Chances are they are going to have to throw away or give away anything left at the end of the day. Garage sales are usually a one-shot event for most sellers. If you are shy and feel uncomfortable bargaining with people, my advice is to jump out of your comfort zone and do it anyway! It won't be nearly as uncomfortable or awkward as you might think. Ask sellers if they will sell their items for lower prices. I am extremely confident you will find the process fun because I know they typically do. Aside from a few exceptions, asking for a better price is not rude. Negotiating is just the way things are done at garage sales, and it is expected. If sellers say no, then fine. Either buy those items or move on. If sellers say yes (and they typically will), you save some money. As I stated earlier, you're saving a few dollars here and there will quickly add up.

Listen to what is going on around you. If you hear other people trying to make a deal and they get shot down, chances are you will too. It's best to save your energy and enthusiasm, so either walk away or pay what the stubborn sellers want. If, on the other hand, you overhear successful deals being made, you can safely assume the particular seller is easy to work with. Most importantly, be pleasant, smile a lot, or in some cases put on a serious face, especially if it's a higher-end item. You will learn rather fast how to deal with each individual seller and item. And yes, you can have a serious face and still be pleasant!

Phrases and Their Meanings
Let's witness a little role-playing, eh? Here are some phrases and scenarios you will hear from sellers, which I will translate and show you

how you should respond. In this scenario, the buyer is polite, and the seller, up until the last example below, is anxious to get rid of things. The buyer asks what the initial asking price is, and the seller may respond with one of the following comments:

Seller: Well, I'd like to get twenty dollars.
>   *Translation: I'd like a lot of things in life, but that doesn't neces-sarily mean I'm going to get them, so make me an offer. I want this thing gone.*

The seller only pauses for some time.
>   *Translation: I really don't know. Make me an offer, and get it out of here.*

Seller: Well, I have been asking for twenty dollars.
>   *Translation: No one is biting. It's late in the day. I'm hot, tired, and getting a little irritated. Just take the darn thing!*

Seller: I don't know. How much do you want to give me?
>   *Translation: Make me an offer, and I'll probably take it.*

Seller: These go for one hundred dollars on eBay.
>   *Translation: I don't want to take the time to sell this on eBay, or I would have. Make me a reasonable offer, and I'm okay with you making a profit. But it had better be reasonable and probably no less than fifty dollars.*

Seller: I'm asking twenty dollars.
>   *Translation: I'm for sure willing to take less because I just said I was asking. Can't you read behind the lines, polite buyer? Just make me an offer!*

Seller: I want twenty dollars!
>   *Translation: Don't even try to bargain with me. Best to pay me or walk. Do not make me an offer.*

The list could go on, but this gives you a working idea on the meaning behind the words. Did you notice that all but one of these transla-tions showed that offers were welcome?

Now how about the polite buyer? What are good phrases and responses for the buyer to use? Here are some of the best responses or opening lines he or she could use.

Buyer: Hmm. [He holds the item in his hand, looking it over carefully.] I don't know…how much?

The buyer simply sounds and looks very unenthusiastic—trust me, the seller will pick up on such behavior and may give it to him for a song.

Buyer: Aye yai yai…do I really want this?

Now he has the seller completely on the defense.

Let's say the seller is asking twenty dollars for an item:

Buyer: (knows he or she will pay fifteen dollars and says in a very humble tone): Can I give you ten dollars?

Seller likes the fact that buyer is polite, so he or she makes a fair counter offer of twelve dollars. Buyer just saved eight bucks off the asking price and three off what he was willing to pay in the first place! This may not sound like a huge savings, but if this kind of negotiation is done all day, the amount saved will be substantial.

Buyer: How much do you want for this thing? [He looks over the vintage, near mint-condition boom box cassette/radio player.]

Buyer has lessened the value of the boom box by calling it "this thing." It would have been a mistake to ask the seller "How much for this vintage boom box?" Even just using the word boom box could have been problematic. Use language that will devalue items, like in this instance where the buyer called the boom box "this thing." In another example, if a polite buyer ran across a collection of something he or she wanted to buy, he or she would refer to it as "all this stuff" not a collection. The word collection might not be the right word to use in a negotiation.

The list could go on, but this should give you a working idea on dialogue. But please note that the seller is indeed the current owner of the item. The buyer has no control over how the seller acts or talks. The polite buyer does not own the item (yet) and is on the seller's property, so the buyer must act and talk as his name suggests—very politely. Rudeness or gruffness almost always results in a bad deal, an experience that is not pleasurable for either party.

Making the Process Fun and Enjoyable for Both Parties

I suspect the main reason you purchased this book was to earn some extra money. There is no denying that money is a great motivating factor. But I am confident you also thought garage sailing could be fun. Earning money doing something enjoyable is quite a remarkable feeling. The renowned and flamboyant pianist Liberace is famous for telling his audience during a show, "I'm having so much fun, I feel guilty taking your money...but I will." If you feel something similar in any pursuit in life, you're onto something good!

Every hobby or business always has negatives or unenjoyable aspects—things you would rather avoid but have to deal with. I don't want that part to be your negotiating with sellers, which will be the main nucleus of your sailing. Bargaining should be one of the most enjoyable aspects. Here are some hints that will help make this process not only fun but exciting.

Playing a Game

Think of it this way: liken garage sailing to some form of a fun card game like poker, either casino gaming or playing cards with friends or family. You know that feeling of excitement right before you are dealt that final card? What are you going to get? How strong will your hand be compared with the other hands? If you really enjoy such aspects of gaming, you will feel a similar sensation while sailing.

Walking up to a garage sale should give you the same feeling you get right before you are dealt your hand. There is a sense of fun and excitement, same as it should be as you walk onto a garage sale. Your hand might be just a pair of deuces, which is not bad, or it might be a full house. But sometimes you are holding a losing hand that you need to walk away from. That's okay; it's just part of the game of garage sailing. In the rarest events, you might hold a royal flush! For instance in 2007, a Chinese bowl was purchased at a garage sale for $3.00. It was later sold at an auction in 2013 for well over $2 million! Although the odds of something like this happening are astronomical, I will say that this person *never* would have found the bowl if he or she were not at a garage sale to begin with!

Approach with a Smile and a Good Attitude
I find it humorous when I pull up to some houses, get out of my car, and walk toward the sales to see the proprietors staring at me with anticipation and welcoming smiles. How often do you get to experience that during an average week, let alone in a day? Understand that in most cases, sellers are just as excited to sell their stuff as you are to buy it. Well maybe not as excited; I'd much rather be a buyer than a seller! The point is, except for the rarest of cases, garage sales are a mutually enjoyed event for both parties; if you simply remember that fact, your experience will be consistently fun. On this same note, the sellers waiting for you will often be little people—kids selling lemonade or cookies. It's your call; sometimes I won't buy anything, but I still try to throw them fifty cents or so. It'll make you feel great. Also, if you give them some money or buy such treats from kids *before* you start looking around, you better believe the moms and dads are going to be easier to deal with.

Meet New People
Here is something else to keep in mind (and we'll refer to this later in the final chapter, "Self-Improvement") to make the experience even more fun and rewarding. Are you looking to meet new people? You may just want to take care of business and move on, and that's okay. Then again, you might be open to making new social contacts. Keep in mind that Saturday garage sales (excluding the first hour or so) are typically a very relaxed atmosphere. For most people, Saturday is a day off. Both sellers and buyers alike have chosen to spend it this

way. Garage sailing is a great way to meet new people because you deal with a captive audience. During slow periods, sellers have nothing to do, so they enjoy engaging in light and pleasant conversation. There are no rules saying you must participate. You might be more interested in getting to another sale. But if perhaps you enjoy talking to and meeting new people or are just trying to come out of your shell a bit, if so, and you are willing to sacrifice a little time and potential profits for it, garage sailing is an absolutely perfect way to do so. Conversation flows very naturally. Perhaps everyone's being out in the sun on a Saturday creates the relaxed atmosphere, or maybe it's the fact that everyone is usually having fun at it. Whatever the case, take advantage of the positivity. You might find your meeting new people will add a wonderful dimension to your sailing hobby. However, it goes without saying that you should avoid engaging in conversations about valuable items you spot—business first, pleasure second!

Should I Feel Guilty?

This is a completely legitimate thought. You go to a sale and meet some wonderful sellers; perhaps their kids are helping with the sale; everyone is having fun, but—Wham!—this wonderful moment is frozen in time as you gaze upon a one-dollar item that you know is easily worth well more than a hundred bucks, or it could even be a much bigger find. Rest assured that these events will happen, as they should, but you may feel guilty in some way, as though you're taking advantage of someone. It may feel even worse if that person is the delightfully friendly type. Now I would rarely if ever tell anyone to feel guilty or not guilty for that matter because I personally believe it is wrong to tell anyone how they should or should not feel. I will, however, provide some thoughts and insights for you that I'm confident should ease your conscience.

Let's consider a sale in which the sellers, Mr. and Mrs. Proprietor, have made a conscious decision to sell their items to the open public. You did not approach the Proprietors; rather they approached you by placing a sign in front of their home to advertise the fact that items are for sale. It would be completely different if you went knocking on doors in older neighborhoods asking the occupants if they had stuff in their garages or attics they would like to sell and then proceeded to buy quality items at ridiculously discounted prices. You are *not* doing this. You are accepting an invitation directly from the seller to peruse certain items.

Also, sellers set the prices, not you. For whatever reason, sellers choose to sell particular items at certain prices. I don't think it is your responsibility to question that. On very rare occasions, a seller may ask you to make an offer for a certain item. In cases like this, I typically just say that I have no idea and kindly ask how much they want for it. But such encounters are extremely rare because again, sellers usually set the prices. In many cases, items already have prices written or tagged on them.

Remember, for the most part, if a seller really wanted to get as much as possible for an item, he or she would have tried to have done so. Obviously, this kind of person wants to avoid going through the hassle of researching value. Keep in mind that in today's age, ascertaining value is very easy to do. Even the rare people who do not own computers or smartphones know others who do. For whatever reason, however, this particular seller did not want to deal with researching value. This seller's chosen loss is your chosen gain.

Exceptions: Do Not Make These Deals
Certainly avoid making deals with minors. Always make sure an adult is involved in any kind of negotiation or purchase. Do not deal with individuals who are under the influence of drugs or alcohol or with anyone else unable to make a rational decision.

Sorry, It's Not for Sale
One time, I was at a sale and noticed some decoy ducks used for hunting, but I was quite sure they were not worth anything. The proprietor said she had a whole bunch of others in her backyard and

proceeded to show me. She was not sure if she was going to sell them or not and asked me if I knew anything about this kind of collectible. I knew enough to know that the ducks in the backyard may have some value. I told her everything she wanted to know and, of course, talked myself out of any kind of potential deal.

Why did I help her? Simply put, my informing her was the right thing to do. She was not trying to sell those backyard ducks. At this time she was only curious about their value, so I told her. Quite honestly, if she had not asked me, I still would have told her. For whatever reason, she was not selling those ducks, and I would have been overstepping my boundaries to try to talk her into selling them.

Now let's say she did have them for sale but still asked me if I knew. That's a tough call and a personal one at that. You would have to look at the whole picture and make whatever moral call you felt was right. Thank goodness that you will rarely be put in that kind of situation, but if so, perhaps you can give them basic information since they asked, and if they still want to sell (and they probably will), you're fine.

For instance one time I came across a guitar with a maker I was not familiar with. I used my smartphone and discovered that one just like it sold for $500; they were asking $100. I really wanted this guitar for myself, not for resale. The sellers told me they had tried and tried to get information on it but could not find it. I simply told them I just did and one had sold for $500.

I personally felt in that situation it was the right thing to do since they told me they were interested in value but had a problem ascertaining it, and I had just found it! I asked if they still wanted to sell it, and they hemmed and hawed a bit. I then told them the absolute truth, that the condition of the other one might have been much better and that with guitars you just never know the condition without an expert looking at it. I told them I would give them $120.00, that's $20.00 more than what they were asking. They accepted, everyone was happy, and guess what? I did take it to an expert and he confirmed there were some issues, minor but still issues all the same. I'm still very happy I bought that guitar and to this day use and enjoy it. I was happy to buy, and they were happy to sell.

Charitable Causes

You will come across a lot of sales that are for some type of charitable cause, perhaps something as common as Boy or Girl Scouts or something as *uncommon* as raising money for a loved one who has cancer or raising funds to help pay for a funeral. Here's my take: you'll have to personally come to terms with your own views on such matters. For normal church sales or fund raisers for common charitable causes, I will usually pay what they're asking and maybe even throw in a few extra bucks if I feel it. For bulk items, such as DVDs, CDs, and books, I still negotiate. If there's nothing I want, I'll sometimes just force myself to find something or perhaps donate a few dollars.

For unique fund-raising sales—that is things like life-or-death matters or funeral funds—I would approach differently. If I see something that's worth some money, and I can make a little profit, I'll just, as I said before, pay what they're asking and add a little. The sellers at these types of sales are grateful to sell anything. In this case I am making very little on these purchases anyway; but if for some reason I sold it and later felt guilty or uncomfortable for whatever reason, then I would just donate some or all of the profits to another cause.

That said, if at the same sale I found a real treasure—let's say a very rare Rolling Stones record album I knew was worth a mint—I would feel obligated to inform the seller of the value. (Thank goodness I've never been tested in that regard!) I personally find that it is just too big of a treasure not to say anything for such a serious cause. Again, the odds of you being put in that position are slim, but whatever you choose to do if you are in that position is your choice.

Questions

Occasionally, sellers will ask you what you plan to do with an item. It is really none of their business in my opinion, but I suppose technically it's their prerogative, but in accordance with making garage sailing a fun experience, here are some of the questions I've been asked and how I suggest you answer them.

"What are you going to do with this?"
"Mind your own darn business!" is what you are going to think. But this is what you are going to verbalize: "I'm not one hundred percent sure. I may keep it, give it away, or even resell it." Say it fast, casually and in a low tone; don't make a big deal out of it.

That's it. You need not say another word, since you have just told them the absolute truth. You may not sell the item. You may later think of someone who could use the item, or you may find it lacks the value you thought it had and end up giving it away to charity. You may find you like the item and decide to keep it. And it is, of course, quite likely you may sell it. These are all viable explanations to that rather inappropriate question. If you think one or more of the options are not true then just leave it out. You can also simply answer their question with "I'm not sure."

"Are you going to sell this on the Internet?"
Yes, I've been asked that straight out, but don't worry it doesn't happen often. Here's what I say: "Maybe, or I might just give it away." Again, if you think you may want to keep it, tell them that too. Be honest, keep your answers short and don't go into any detail. They will quickly realize you really don't want to talk about it.

"What are you going to do with all of these? Are you some kind of dealer?"
This pair of questions comes up occasionally when I'm buying an entire lot of something, often with DVDs, CDs, and books. This is a good response: "Well, I'll probably end up keeping some, giving some away, and selling some." And that is what happens often after I buy a lot of DVDs, CDs and books. Think about it. The same may be true for you; if so, tell them the truth.

Another answer to some of the above questions, which shuts them up almost every time and in which you are not lying, is "These are not for me. They're for someone else."

That answer works better for individual items, but it does work. I use this one the most. The truth is that the item is not for you; it is for someone else. But the seller does not need to know that you don't know who that someone else is and that it is someone who is going to buy it online. All the seller needs to know is that it's for someone else—end of story. Quite honesty it is their possession and I suppose they have the right to ask anything they want, but within the world of garage sales I feel that their questions are quite inappropriate but I certainly don't let it agitate me.

In truth, it's relatively rare that a seller will ask questions. People generally don't care, and they're too busy doing other things like trying to hold a garage sale! Again, such questions pop up more when I buy an entire lot of items, but even then, they are the exception, not the rule.

Just Three Little Hints

First, don't look too intently at an item you are interested in. Just casually pick it up and maybe glance at some other stuff. Be very casual, but if you covet a particular item, *do not* put it down. Keep it in your hands; otherwise, anyone else can grab it. Just behave as though you are going back and forth in your head, deciding whether you even want it.

Secondly, remember: be casual, casual, casual! Relax. Scratch your head. Chances are the proprietor may even see your indecisiveness and offer you a deal you can't refuse, right then and there. Don't answer too quickly, but shrug your shoulders a little bit and say, "Sure, why not?"

Finally, if you are going to go through a bunch of DVDs, CD's, books or really any group of multiple similar items, ask how much before you start going through them. For one if the price is too high you will have wasted valuable time going through all that stuff only to find out AFTER that it's overpriced. But another probably more important factor is if you have already found things you want to buy *and then* ask the price, you have lost some leverage. The seller already knows you have somethings that interest you. Try to ask first if you can.

Utilizing Your Smartphone

Although I've brought up the use of a smartphone earlier, I want to go into more specifics about the power and potential of this device. Not too many years ago, I would have to use my gut alone when buying items. I had no guaranteed way to discern whether the items I was about to buy had value or not. I had to wait until I got home to find out. You will note that in many instances the following chapters 5 through 8 are written in such a way as if you do *not* own a smartphone. This will help you gain a working knowledge of value. There will be times when using your smartphone will not be an option. You will either have to buy an item now or not, but in most cases, your trusted smartphone is going to be your best friend. I generally use eBay when checking in the field. I simply downloaded an eBay app on my smartphone. When I see an item that I think has value, I can check eBay to find out what similar items have sold for.

When using your smartphone to research the value of an item, try not to be too conspicuous; that is, don't let the seller or other buyers realize you are onto something. Just walk away from the crowds of people and off to the side or safely toward the street and if appropriate holding the item. People will probably think you're just returning a text or something. If the item is too heavy to hold in your hands while you're researching it, and you must put it down, then do so, you have no choice. You only need a couple of minutes, if that, to research.

When I check eBay, I type in the item with basic information, refining my search to only sold items, and refine my search again to the highest items first. I then check to see if the price is a trend for this particular item. If I find one item that sold for a high price and a number of others that sold very low, then I need to question my decision to buy or not.

Your memory will serve you well and eventually is going to get better. Let's say you see an old turntable from the seventies or eighties, for instance a Marantz 6300 turntable. What you don't want to do is sit in front of it with your smartphone and look it up while the proprietor or anyone for that matter watches you. You will need to hone your memory skills and remember Marantz 6300. Walk away casually, as if you would if you need to make a call or text someone. Type in 6300 first (I personally find it is easier to remember names than numbers) and then type in Marantz. If you are comfortably far enough away from everyone and you have a voice activation feature on your smartphone you can simply use that. Do your research as stated above. In this case, you will see that this particular turntable can easily fetch more than $500, and there are plenty of closed auctions that can back that up. Put your smartphone away, and do not rush back to the item. Just casually find your way to the Marantz, and go from there.

If you cannot find anything on eBay, do a Google search; you may see something in your search that shows value. If you still cannot find anything (which is quite uncommon), you need to make a judgment call. My suggestion: buy it as long as it is not overly priced. It could be very rare, which is perhaps why you are having difficulty finding it.

For the most part, you will be in direct sunlight, and it can be at times difficult viewing your screen. Talk with your smartphone carrier about ways to reduce glare.

Be polite; avoid checking your smartphone right in the middle of a sale. You are going to get in other people's way, and it may be obvious to the proprietor that you are researching one of their items. Some sellers might not like that. They do not want to feel as though they are underselling something. Just casually walk away from the sale as if you are doing personal business, which you are!

You have now learned enough to negotiate effectively and in a way that is fun, simple, and direct. The more you do it, the more comfortable you'll feel and the more natural it will flow. Learning how to negotiate for a particular item is one thing, but now you need to figure out what items are worth the effort of negotiating. The next few chapters provide some simple and comprehensive strategies to help you spot these treasures.

Prelude to Chapters 5–8
Some of you may already have a working knowledge of one or many facets of antiques, vintage stuff, collectibles, and so on. That's great; you're way ahead of the game, and I'm very glad! But that said, you may read on and think, "Hey, you completely missed the part about such and such when referencing vintage items!" Or, "Wait, you didn't even mention primitive art from the turn of the century in your antique section!" (By the way, primitive art can be defined as cultural artifacts of ethnic groups deemed to have a relatively low standard of techno-logical development by Western standards…Always learning!)

My answer to that is, "Yes, I am completely aware that there are many missing links so to speak in the following sections and really in other parts of this book as well. This was done consciously and for a rea-son." Although this book has huge benefit and value for everyone, professional, novice, and amateurs alike, I suspect most people who purchased this book know little, if anything, about these subjects, which is the perfect reason to have bought it in the first place, so if you are one of those people then congrats!

My goal is to make this simple and fun yet profitable for *anyone* to do and not something reserved only for persons with a working knowledge of value. Had I written this book in any other way, I fear heads would start spinning very early on and that my book would end up unread and sitting in a box at someone's garage sale! I did not want that to happen. I truly wanted you, my reader, to succeed at sailing. To make money, have fun, and not get frustrated in the pro-cess but rather to continually learn at a comfortable pace. That said, are you ready? Let's have some fun and talk about antiques, vintage stuff, and collectibles!

5

Antiques, Vintage Stuff, and Collectibles: How to Recognize Value

I **WOULD SAY** that most people are unaware that they have the ability to spot valuable items at a garage sale. They are fully convinced that this purported talent is reserved for antique dealers and the like. In one sense, they are correct. If you're considering opening up an antique store or collectible shop, you better know what you are doing. If you plan to bid on high-price art, manuscripts, and antiquities, it only makes sense to possess professional experience and knowledge of this field. In your case, however, you won't perform any of these tasks; rather, you will simply drive around on Saturdays, searching for items that you can resell on the Internet for fun and profit—that's it. Some simple and basic rules exist that I am convinced will enable anyone, and I mean anyone, to waltz onto a garage sale and, within minutes, know if there might be value peering out from amid an array of junk.

I am not a professional antique dealer; I have some experience with certain collectibles, but I am not in any sort of collectible business, so to speak. I do not make my living from buying and selling rare and hard-to-find artifacts. I do not attend high-end auctions. I don't own a collectible or antique store, nor do I want to. I am providing you with simple to the point basics. This book was written by an amateur for other amateurs not antique and collectible dealers or students of that industry. That said, let's move on.

The Internet has enabled collectors to find their prizes with simple clicks of a mouse. Some of you, like me, may remember the pre-Internet days. If someone wanted a particular collectible, they would have to subscribe to certain magazines or advertise in a local paper or make dozens of phone calls to antique and collectible stores all over the country or even the world for that matter.

This most certainly is not the case now. Anytime, twenty-four hours a day, we can sit in front of our computer or smartphone and, within less than a minute or two, have a list of choice collectibles right at our fingertips and often at great prices. It may be cliché to say that this is the age of knowledge and that the future is now, but the sometimes frightening but mostly exciting fact is that there is a load of truth in that cliché: opportunity is a simple click away, and because of it, the sky is the limit.

A certain question, however, is probably nagging your mind: How can I, someone who knows absolutely nothing about antiques, vintage stuff, and collectibles, even begin to think I can do this?

Truthfully, that is a very legitimate question and concern. The answer is that you most definitely can, and I'll be explaining how. First, here's a little hint, one of the tricks of the trade, if you will. However, bear in mind this is *not* a necessary component to making your garage-sailing venture successful, but it will definitely help. Buy antique and collectibles price guides (with photos) that are used but not terribly old. You can get them on Amazon or eBay for a song. So many varied types of antiques, vintage stuff, and collectibles are out there, and things you wouldn't even imagine to have value are indeed demanded by collectors worldwide. Having these books for reference purposes or just to browse through will empower you with knowledge and give you a subconscious idea of what to keep your eye on at garage sales.

In regard to this book and this chapter, look at the information as *CliffsNotes* into buying and selling antiques, vintage stuff, and collectibles. You will be taught the very basics of what to look for, but other more detailed books will go into much more detail. You can proceed successfully without other reference books, but they will help you establish a more well-rounded knowledge, as well as a keener eye. In addition and perhaps more realistically, just play around on the Internet and look up auctions on various types of items. You will be surprised at how fast you become good at detecting the value of things you find at garage sales!

Before we begin, we need to establish a few simple definitions, and I do mean simple. I have purposely kept this part of the book as easy and focused as possible. Here's why: in the context of human nature, if tasks become too complex, people tend to shy away from them, especially if those tasks become too much like work. Volumes can be written on antiques, vintage stuff, and collectibles; there is no definite end. Your purpose is to be able to spot potential value—that's it. The Internet will do the job of appraising and selling the item. If you want to become especially interested in a particular type of collectible, you would expand your knowledge by investing in books, classes, or seminars. However, if your sole purpose is to have some fun and make a profit by going to garage sales, this book (in my humble opinion) is all you need. The other books will only help you but are not a necessity for our purposes. Let's address the characteristics of antiques vintage stuff and collectibles quickly and easily and then move forward.

What Is an Antique?

There are some interesting views on this subject, but the consensus seems to be that an antique is more than one hundred years old. If you stick with that, you should be safe. You can use the following information to help you spot *all* old items, antique or not, but for easier reading we are simply going to refer to items in this section as antiques. You can usually recognize an antique the minute you see it because of one simple reason: it is old, and it looks it! Items of yesteryear typically have a certain look. Let's use people as an example. Old people usually look a certain way. They act, talk, and walk a certain way. Like people, antique items are very easy to spot. An elderly person will use particular words in his or her daily vocabulary that are outdated.

For example;

One's great-grandfather might shyly mention that "a boy and a girl were courting with each other."

One's grandfather might mutter, "That young man and lady are keeping company."

One's father might say, "How nice it is that those two kids are going steady."

And we might say, "Those two are dating, going on ten years now!"

My point is that each generation can be spotted by the language it uses.

Elderly people typically carry themselves in a certain way. Their aging limbs are not what they used to be, and their fragility comes out in the way they stand, sit, and walk. There are the telltale signs of gray hair, wrinkled skin, and loss of hearing. The point I want to make is very basic: you do not need to be a geriatric doctor to recognize that someone is old; nor do you need to be an antique dealer to spot an antique or any old collectible or vintage item.

How to Spot Antiques

When establishing age, keep in mind that just like people, items and their ages can be spotted by certain characteristics of their era. You just need to know what to look for. When you see an antique, you usually know it right away. It does not have some of the attributes of more modern items. The following sections cover some basic details that will help you discern the age of items and antiques.

Metal
Yes, there was a time when plastic did not exist in mass production. Toys, small kitchen appliances, and so forth—the list is endless. Many things were made of metal or cast in iron and very heavy. If you have an item composed of heavy metal but know it generally comes in plastic, it could be an antique. Here's a perfect example: Today, toys are generally made of plastic, but yesteryear's toys were metal and quite heavy. Not all of today's toys are plastic—some are made of metal. But when you're holding a metal toy that is not an antique, you'll notice it has an obvious shine and general polish. Also, check out the printing or copyright markings. You will find that common sense is a strong age meter when it comes to discerning the old from the new.

Any metal on an antique item can be rusted, dull, or worn. You may note pitting in the metal. Just rub your finger across the surface; if the texture is rough and gritty or has collected dust and rust, that's a great sign you're holding an antique. If the texture feels smooth, that could also be a sign that the item is old: either it has gone untouched, or more likely been used a lot in its day, resulting in a worn, smooth, metallic feel. In some cases, many of these signs can apply to the same item. If the metal shines and reflects light well, it might not be an antique but a reproduction. Antiques usually have more of a dull yet decorative look to them. For instance, antique hinges often have an almost fancy look in their appearance, with lots of attention to detail, but they really don't sparkle. Modern items can be rather shiny, plain, and almost antiseptic.

Wood
Antique wood often has a rich, dark, and aged look to it. It may also have lots of nicks and scratches, but note if the scratches seem new.

Typically, the nicks and scratches on antique items look and feel dull. A newer scratch can imply that the item has been in recent use, as opposed to sitting in someone's attic or garage for many decades. A newer scratch is also rough to the feel and sharp in its look, but an older scratch has become part of the item, in a sense. The scratch is present but worn to the point that it is there but almost flush with the wood. Wooden items may also have more rounded edges instead of sharp ones, a sign the item has seen a lot of use but not for quite some time.

Patina
This is a word you will come across often when reviewing antique auctions. You may also be using it while describing items you are selling. This is something you will be keeping an eye out for. For our purposes patina is a surface appearance of something that has grown beautiful with age and/or its use. It's tough to replicate. Age has naturally turned the once new item into something likened to a very old and well-aged bottle of wine. Simply put, patina is beautiful; it has a very rich and endearing warmth look to it. It has been well used over the years but not abused, and for the most part has not seen much, if any use in many, many years. You'll sometimes come across items that have patina at a garage sale. You will know it when you see it; you will almost "feel" it. Patina is in my opinion one of the best things that can happen to an item over the years. Real old people who are warm and friendly and not bitter have what I call personality patina. It is very difficult to describe as is often the challenge when trying to put a description on anything of beauty.

Paper
If it's a paper-related item, the paper could seem brittle, yellowed, and very fragile. Paper antiques are unique in many cases. It's not so much the item as it is what is written or drawn on the item that has value. Bubble-gum cards are a good example. If the card represents

a modern-era sports hero, there may be some value to it, but it's clearly not an antique. If you find the same card made with the same material except it looks old and worn and depicts one of yesterday's heroes from a hundred years ago, then you may have an antique and quite possibly a valuable item on your hand.

Paper items can be tricky. On one hand, they were typically produced in abundance, but on the other hand, they perished very easily. Paper products are a weak opponent against the elements. Air can wither paper, and water and fire will destroy it. Thus, most of the antique paper products that have survived to the present were probably stored safely—for example, in a box in someone's attic, basement, or garage—but even then, these paper-based items were susceptible to things like vermin, bugs, or mold and mildew. So many different types of paper products exist that it would be impossible to begin listing what they are. But there are many such items out there. Just to give you an idea, here are some examples of paper products that could have value: postcards, old magazines, matchbooks, photographs, prints, movie posters, and the list goes on and on.

I want you to try to understand that all aspects of life of yesteryear can be valuable. Whatever you find, if that little voice inside of you (which will get clearer with time) tells you there may be value in a particular item, just buy it, especially if it is cheap enough; typically, it will be. Even if such items end up being worthless, the small amount of capital you spend is a sort of investment, adding to your expertise and knowledge in your new hobby. A paper product does not necessarily have to be in great condition to make it valuable. Since there were so many of these items destroyed over the years, it is understandable if these items show some wear; it goes with the territory of being a combustible and delicate item.

Fabric

Fabric is very similar to paper: it's very perishable but not as much as paper. One of the more common detrimental foes to fabric can be staining or wear. For example, some vintage luggage can be a high-demand collectible these days. It is somewhat common to find general wear, so the value is still there. Of course, an old designer suitcase from the thirties that was barely used and has been sitting in someone's closet for fifty to seventy-five years is a real find! Other examples of fabric items to search for are purses, hats, and various types of clothing. Flip through pricing guidebooks of antiques and collectibles and/or do Internet searches. Once again, doing so is not a must, but it is a great training aid for the mind.

In regard to clothing, you can easily establish age by the look of the article. If you found an article of men's clothing that not only looked old and a bit tattered but also looked like it was something you had seen worn in a movie taking place during World War I, then you can pretty much assume it probably is from that era. If you come across a flowing Victorian dress with lots of frills, you should know you probably have a turn-of-the-century piece.

You can detect the ages of other fabric items also by the obvious look of the era in which it was made. Again, vintage luggage as an example, aside from it's obvious age, has a definite uniqueness that would stand out from today's luggage. As I have mentioned, you will find that ordinary common sense is a powerful force when it comes to discerning age and value. But there are also online resources that can help you identify older items. Let's use clothing as yet another example; some online resources will help identify the age of clothing from simply the style or wording of the labels.

Folk Art

Just like all other categories in this book, this subject can be quite extensive, but let's simplify describing it for our needs. Folk art is that which is handmade, typically by peasants, tradespeople, or artisans, really the less affluent social class. A lot of this is quite collectible and valuable. For the most part, much of what you need to be concerned with are crafty type of things: woodcraft, embroidery or leatherwork for instance, ceramics, jewelry, stained glass windows, and so forth. Old paintings can be a form of folk art too. To make it a little easier on you, just pretend you are at an arts and craft show. That's a feel of what I want you to be on the look for, the only difference is that the "craft" handmade things that you are going to buy at garage sales has all the markings of being an older piece.

Some of the folk art you run across may include the name of the artist; there can be a great following for them. Let's take a crafter or of wooden animals for example; sometimes their name will appear etched or written at the bottom of the piece. This could be a great find and will make it much easier for you to ascertain value. Often, however, there is no name, but that does not mean it has no worth only that it may be a bit challenging to place a value on it. This is an area that could be a bit problematic for you when trying to figure out what to list it for, or if it is even worth anything. Not impossible mind you but ultimately time consuming trying to find items that look like it because folk art certainly has a "one of a kind" feel to it and really, that's pretty much what they are, one of a kind.

Therefore, to cut down on your losses, I would recommend that if an item has no name on it but looks to be old, kind of how we articulated in the "How to Spot Antiques" section, and looks to be handcrafted, just buy it; if the price is too high then chances are the proprietor already did some checking and has an idea of value. If they even utter the word *folk art* coupled with a higher price, then walk away.

Are there more modern folk art items? Why yes. However, it might be a bit more challenging to ascertain age, unless you can see an indication of an era. Let's take hippies for instance; crafts they made in the sixties and seventies can be good finds. You won't miss the telltale signs of the era, like flowers, psychedelic colors, or a peace sign. If you find something like this and it seems a bit worn or fragile, then you could have an authentic piece of hippie folk art in your possession.

Let the seller's quoted price tell you more about whether to buy folk art or not. If it's real inexpensive, like a few bucks, you're good. But let's take the hippie stuff as an example. If the seller says something like "Oh, I want at least thirty-five dollars for this cool piece,"

then I'd probably advise walking or at the least thinking very seriously about even making an offer. If they say "I want fifty dollars for
this piece of 1960s hippie folk art," then unless you are privy to more
knowledge about value than the seller I would recommend you run!
By the way, this is a perfect example in my opinion of a collectible
that is somewhat affordable now but may not be in the next decade
or two. Always keep an eye out for investments for yourself.

Again, folk art can be problematic in identifying, but it can also be
a very fun and challenging hunt on your Saturdays not to mention
quite equitable.

Fragile: Handle With Care!
Be careful when you are handling old, fragile items. They are not
yours (yet); I have found some beautiful pieces of the past that have
been preserved for decades upon decades. The preservation is often
due to very little if any human contact. Suddenly, this wonderful,
shy, introverted, and protected gem gets cast in among newer and
more extroverted pieces of granite bullies—figuratively speaking, of
course. Such items are then displayed to the general public at seven
in the morning. We humans sometimes have a nasty way of wanting
to put our hands on everything. Unfortunately, we sometimes touch
and handle something harshly that we should treat very gently. What
a shame to see these preciously preserved items that have survived
decades of wars, depressions, and societal changes be manhandled
and hurt in such a short period of time—that is, on one brief Saturday
morning or afternoon. Garage-sale guests are not the only culprits;
the proprietors of sales can also cause damage to these items, and
quite often they do. Without thinking, they just throw such treasures
among junk or toss them on their lawns, which are often layered with
morning dew. They may commit the horrible atrocity of (especially if
it's a paper product) putting a sticky price tag on such items or, even
worse, writing the prices on them with ink!

Neglected Items, Makeovers, and Reproductions

If you find items that fit the above descriptions, have you definitely found an antique or really old item? No. Let's talk about people again as an example. Have you ever met someone who looks decades older than he or she is because of bad habits, sickness, stress, or genes? We all have met such people. That could be the same scenario with something you find that looks older than it really is. There are no hard-and-fast rules to spotting antiques for amateurs; we just have to put the odds in our favor. Sometimes antiques have had a makeover; that's right, just as some older people have. It is very rare that you'll run into an antique that's been refurbished at a garage sale, but doing so could happen.

There are two schools of thought about renovated items. Buyers who like the look of renovated items and don't care as much about authenticity generally prefer the makeover look. True collectors, however, typically prefer such items to be in their most original shape possible, even though that may mean the items are not as visually pleasant. This type of collector finds more beauty in the originality than the renovation.

Again, refurbished items are a very uncommon find at garage sales, but you will find many reproductions. A reproduction has an antique look to it. But how do you know if it's a reproduction? Here's the easiest, fastest, and best way to discern if an antique is real or fake: ask the owner! You're at a garage sale. These are just average people. They are typically honest and forthright. They're not out to rip anyone off; they just want to get rid of their extra stuff.

You'll probably be able to tell on your own. A reproduction is usually not very detailed. It looks like an item that is new and old at the same time. In general, you will not find scratches, dings, or markings. In many cases, a reproduction has some kind of printed or stamped information on it—the maker, copyright information, or sometimes even the year it was made. In general, such printing or stamps of identification are visually sharp, a dead giveaway that item is a reproduction. Again, if you have any questions, just ask the seller. There may be some value for reproductions; often they do as stated above have information on it, so it's easy to reference on your smartphone.

What Are Collectibles?

An antique is one hundred years old or more, but how old should a collectible be? There are no definite criteria for identifying age. Simply stated, a collectible is an object someone chooses to collect as a hobby. It does not have to be old. Many people collect the newest releases of model cars or dolls; they are certainly thought of as collectibles, but they are not old. True, many collectibles are items of the past, but age is not a defining factor.

Let's say someone collects military buttons from the Civil and Revolutionary Wars. What this person has hanging on the wall is a collection of antique military buttons. If a different person collects military buttons from the Korean or Vietnam era, he or she is displaying old collectible military buttons. Both sets of buttons fall into the same category, but age has turned one into an antique. Each set is technically a collectible because each is made of objects someone chooses to collect as a hobby. But the older set is antique. What if someone had a collection of buttons from the most recent Olympic Games? This person is displaying a newer collectible. My point is that all three can be categorized as a collectible.

You will find that collectibles are going to be a huge part of your garage sailing, more so than antiques. Many collectibles can be much more affordable to the average buyer than antiques. People out there have all sorts of interests. Collecting is a personal endeavor. Some people may get huge joy out of collecting jelly jars, while others are more traditional in their choosing to collect such things as coins or stamps. Thousands of different types of collectibles are in demand, so your finding them at garage sales will be less difficult than you might assume. Even you probably have loads of such items just sitting in your garage, attic, closet, or basement.

What Is a Vintage Item?

Although there are many vague opinions of what vintage is or is not, for the purposes of this book, we will refer to vintage as an older item that has a recognized and enduring interest, importance, or quality. The key aspect is the enduring interest and quality. For example, take the 1965 Mustang car; it's old, recognizable, has enduring interest, and has a quality that many automobiles of its time did not have. It is a vintage high-in- demand car. Many 1970s Mustangs were only a few years younger, but I personally would be hard pressed to refer to some of them as vintage.

So how does all this affect you? You probably won't be going after cars, but you will buy many vintage items. So for the sake of this book, we are simply going to refer to vintage as older, with lasting and enduring interest.

The bottom line is that vintage is a good thing. People love the word and connotations. They would rather buy a vintage model toy plane than an "old" model toy plane.

So for the sake of keeping it simple, let's just leave it at that; at this juncture in your new hobby it's really all you need to know.

Vintage Stuff from the 1970s–1980s

Although there is plenty of vintage items from previous decades, I want to zero in on this era because there are still, relatively speaking, plenty of items from this era out there and the demand for this type of collectible is increasing. Just like I alluded to at the beginning of this book regarding providing a list of salable items, vintage stuff from the seventies and eighties is seemingly endless. Early video games for example were beginning to erupt on the market, changing the way children (and adults) spent their free time.

How about Television? Huge! Many sitcoms were a household topic (remember, at the time cable TV as we know it today was not influencing households' choices of things to watch). Families were in a way held captive by the limited choices and limited stations. Culture was changing and fast—music, movies, and so forth. Now the eighties in my opinion were like the seventies on steroids. Much of that technology that was beginning to erupt, very much erupted in the eighties.

Again, I'm not big in providing lists because I feel it will limit you; I want to make sure you are open to a variety of finds that will yield you a great return. That said, to just help you get an idea here are some items from that era that are collectible today.

Gaming systems: Both the games and the console can be great finds. Atari, Sega, and Nintendo are some of the more recognizable names.

Cassette players: Walkman cassette players or really any cassette player from that era could be very collectible. Find a boom box radio and cassette player from that era and you may very well be in the money.

Star Trek and *Star Wars* memorabilia: it's becoming increasingly rare and difficult to find, and it can be a challenge to discern original from all the remakes that have ensued since the birth of that culture-changing TV show and movie, so be careful on this one.

TV show memorabilia: Shows like *Dukes of Hazard,* as just one example, had a huge array of marketing items that were made. Everything from the obvious toy cars to blankets. All you have to do is search online for a list of TV shows from this era and you will *not* be without something to keep your eyes on!

Board games: The more obscure the better. By the way, this is a perfect example of how vintage items can overlap onto each other, attracting more than one type of collector. In other words a collector of board games and a collector of television memorabilia will both be interested in a *Dukes*

of Hazard board game. Thus greatly increasing the demand for the item.

Children's toys: There are so, so many of them! Matchbox cars,
dolls, racing sets, G.I. Joes, Evel Knievel merchandise, and
on and on and on!

Eight-Track players: One of my personal favorites. Some of
these were made into more of a nostalgic piece. I once
found an eight-track player that looked like a dynamite
box; as you push down on it, it changed the tracks. Very
collectible and really cool to look at!

It's almost pointless to expand on this too much and again quite honestly limiting. Keep in mind many of the children from the seventies
and eighties (overlapping into the nineties) are all grown up now.
Many want to relive part of their childhood, and collecting this genre
of memorabilia is very affordable for them. This in my opinion is a
great investment. Keep in mind the kids of that era are not at retirement age yet and probably don't have loads of extra money lying
around, but in a few years, they may, and when that happens they're
going to be desiring this stuff even more because now it's all that
much further from their childhood *and* they'll have the extra cash to
invest. It might be a good idea to hang on to some of this type of vintage collectible as an investment for yourself!

Are you from that era? Then you know what I'm talking about. Are
you much younger and a lot of this seems Greek? That's okay! Look,
none of us were around at the turn of the century, but we can all
learn what is collectible from that era, right?

Have fun at this; it's very exciting (and profitable), and let's face
it, you have a much better chance of finding a Mr. Potato Head at
a garage sale than a daguerreotype from the eighteen hundreds!
(A daguerreotype is a photograph taken by an early photographic
process employing an iodine-sensitized silvered plate and mercury
vapor.) See how in sailing you are constantly learning something!

How to Spot Collectibles

You may be thinking, "Thousands of different kinds of collectibles are out there. Where do I even start?" Here are some ideas that will give you valuable clues on how to spot collectibles and which ones to buy.

Newer Collectibles

Newer collectibles are abundant. Like newer Disney collectibles for example; you'll see a decent amount of that out there. Stay away from them, unless of course you have chosen that path of interest. What you're really looking for is the hard-to-find item, the kind of thing that's been thrown away or damaged throughout the years. A Justin Bieber lunch box that is only a few years old could be considered a collectible to the right person but currently lacks much value, but perhaps in time it will have value; we just can never say for sure. Conversely, a forty or so year old Partridge Family lunch box has definite value, even though far fewer people know who The Partridge Family is, as opposed to one of today's mega famous teen idols. If you think an object is less than twenty or so years old, it's probably best to stay away from it.

Older Collectibles

The easiest and most accurate way to discern the age of a collectible is easier than you may think. Although the following aspect may not work for every type of collectible, I am confident that it will work most of the time and pay you huge dividends in the long run. A collectible's age can be judged simply by the era it represents. For example, if you are buying something such as a collectible household item in its original box and on that box is a picture of a woman with a beehive hairdo or a man with long side burns, then you have just been given a huge tip as to the age of this item. This may seem simplistic, but you will see that your identifying an item's original era works for many kinds of collectibles out there. It is the most powerful tool you can possess as you fumble through dozens of items. Older collectibles also have a faded look to them. They lack the sparkle, luster, and shine that newer items have.

Popularity

Being common takes away the excitement of the whole meaning of collecting something. Collectors want what is hard to find and typically avoid the easily obtainable items. There are so many unknown genres of collecting, including merchandise relating to personalities most people have never even heard of, some of which are very rare and valuable. Popular products and characters on the other hand got a lot of adulation, which resulted in mass production of marketing items thus decreasing value.

Here's an example. When I first started garage sailing, I would see stacks of old records in their original covers and in great condition. I would buy some, and then after I got home, I would start my researching only to find most were worthless. Such records had everything going for them: they were older, very pleasing to look at, had pictures of famous people on them, and were in great condition. What seemed to be the problem? The answer is quite simple: I found so many of these things because so many had been made. If I found these with ease, so could other people. Does that mean all records are worthless? Of course not. Some extremely valuable records are out there, not only uncommon records by artists who are unknown to most and had a limited production run, but also from popular artists who also may have had a limited production run on certain albums or who released records before they were famous, which gives you both popularity and scarcity.

I partly brought up records for a reason. I want you to be aware of the passing of time as it relates to value. When I first started doing this, there was as I previously stated, stacks upon stacks of them— not so much these days. Some records that were not desirable a few years ago, have become very collectible; in addition, a new generation of music enthusiasts are now actually not just collecting old record albums but listening to them. They're called audiophiles, and they find a better quality of sound with records than with CDs. In only a few years, records went from basically being sold by the pound to being more collectible than I could have predicted. It has also become popular to frame album covers as artwork.

As I stated earlier, if something is really popular, chances are that related products were produced in mass quantities. But sometimes that same popular entity had a product that was not produced in mass quantity; in that case, you may have a collectible that is a winner. For example, the Beatles were extremely popular, but whether you liked their music or not is irrelevant; their fame and notoriety were unmatched. Does this mean that every Beatles item is valuable? Surprisingly, not everything with the word *Beatles* on it has huge value. For example, it would be an understatement to say that their records were mass produced. Unless you have one of the rarer releases or a near-mint album, chances are you have one of the millions of relatively collectible but not highly valuable Beatles records. Popularity results in mass production, which can in turn equate to little or no value in today's market.

But let's get back to lunch boxes for a minute. Did you know that in the midsixties, Beatles lunch boxes were made? Mostly young girls would proudly tote them to school. Now flash forward to the present, and you find yourself standing in someone's yard, holding a Beatles lunch box. You just found a very valuable item. Why? Because the lunch box is a mix of popularity and relative scarcity.

Let's take it a step further with regard to popularity and scarcity. We all know the Beatles released millions of records, but did you know there was also a Beatles record player released to play all those millions of records? This item is not "relatively" scarce like the aforementioned lunch box; rather it is unbelievably scarce and can be worth thousands because it combines popularity, immense scarcity, and desirability in a tangible form—a huge winner and a great find! By the way, I'm using the Beatles record player as an example. It's highly unlikely you will find one, but you never know with garage sailing. If you do, write to me!

Mint Items

There is a monstrous difference between new and mint items. A fifty-year-old item could be mint, but is certainly not new. When I say *new*, I mean items that were made recently—in the last few years or so. There are times when you may see an old item that looks new. Grab it! The value difference between a good-condition and a mint-condition item is enormous, almost obnoxious, a fact that brings us back to supply and demand. Just how many mint fishing reels from the fifties are out there? I can tell you from experience there are very few. Fishing reels were made to be used, and that they were. But every now and then, someone had a fishing reel that he or she never used and in some cases the person never even took it out of its box! There you have a mint item worth an amount ridiculously higher than the same reel that is in great condition but used. You may also note that even though an item is mint, it will not necessarily look new. It may not have that sparkle and shine. This is good; it will help you to authenticate age. Here's another great example, board games. Some are very rare, but some are quite common; however, find an older but common board game still sealed and you probably have a prize. Find a rare one still sealed and you have a treasure!

Perishability

Another thing to look for in collectibles is perishability. These are items that were easily discarded, destroyed, or thrown away. For example, an original Shirley Temple doll can be worth quite a bit of money, but the same doll in the original box is worth a huge amount more. Even the box without the doll is worth quite a bit. The reason is simple: the box usually got thrown away; it was perishable. Collectors *love* to have what other people do not have. It's probably the number-one trait that most, if not all, hobbyists have in common. They want to own the bragging rights to something. They thoroughly enjoy having the hard-to-find items, those that the majority of fellow collectors fail to attain. Also, most collectors like their prizes to be as complete as possible. They want that Shirley Temple doll, the box it came in, the tags from the store it was purchased at, and even the receipt if possible!

Buy It and Buy It Quick
You should buy any older item that you have not seen before if the price is within a reasonable range. Chances are that such items are rare and hard to find, which is why you don't recognize them. Have you ever seen a wooden plane propeller that's too big for a model and too small for a plane? Neither had I before I found one. I bought it for five bucks, and it ended up being a propeller for an unmanned plane, a drone, used right around or after World War II. I sold it for about a hundred dollars. And it was quite beat up. By the way, that was some years ago; my suspicion is that it would sell for much more in today's market.

You should buy any item that looks to be more than twenty or so years old and is in mint condition, whether you've seen it a million times or not. Remember, like with the aforementioned board games, that a mint aspect is rare, even among some of the most common and abundant items. Take it a step further, if an item was originally produced sealed and you find it that way, then it's taking mint to a whole new level!

Lesson Learned
Over time, you will start to achieve a sense of what has value and what does not. As you start to purchase things and find out they're worthless, you'll know simply not to purchase them again. No harm, no foul. The item probably only costs you a few dollars anyway. Learning lessons in garage sailing is very, very inexpensive. In most other business ventures and hobbies, you'll find mistakes to be extremely costly. Not so in sailing. Mistakes are cheap.

I would have to write an encyclopedia even to begin to list what is collectible and what is worthless. All I can do is give you an idea, a sort of skeleton outline, of what to look for. Over time, you will begin to recognize things that are bombs and things that are "da bomb"!

Things to Avoid
Here are some examples that should help you understand what I mean, and this list could go on. I want to name just a few items to help give you an idea about the kind of thing I am referring to.

Kitchenware
Avoid kitchenware unless you are someone who knows about or desires to learn about it; if that is or could be your niche then go for it, you'll have a lot of inventory to choose from! Aside from that exception, guess what? Humans have always eaten so consider staying clear of plates, glasses, utensils and the such, there's just A LOT of it out there! Yes, you may be overlooking a great deal, but my goal is to help you find salable items quickly without having to weed through hundreds of potentials to find a single treasure. The issue is time management.

What would be the exception? How about ice-cream makers? In days gone by everyone used knives and forks or I'd like to think so, but did everyone have ice-cream makers? Absolutely not—it was unessential to existence. Thus, there is a limited supply of old ice-cream makers. This does not mean that everyday products lack value. Some utensil sets and tableware are worth a bundle, but you're not putting the odds in your favor if you start buying all the old forks, knives, plates, and glassware you see.

Tools
Avoid tools. So many are out there, but there is always the exception. You'll find a few axes out there, but find one made by a company called Norlund Hudson Bay and you may have a prize. Some of those can fetch $500 to $1,000. By the way, I have never found one, probably because I rarely spent much time looking through the piles of tools out

there. I know this from the research I do. Research, research, research! It will no doubt increase your odds of recognizing value and in a big way. This brings me to another extremely important point that you will note has been brought up repeatedly (and for a reason) in this book and that is having a niche or even multiple niches. Nothing should stop you from excelling in one or more genres of collectibles and antiques. For example, as I stated earlier, if you start researching and studying glassware, tools, records, or whatever, you will become more knowledgeable than the average person and, consequently, more successful in your garage sailing. With sound knowledge, you can sift through dozens of items quickly to find the rare treasures, pushing your efficiency far beyond the meager skills of average garage sailors. You can develop your expertise as much as you desire.

Large and Heavy Items
Try to avoid large and heavy items. I once bought a very old children's tricycle. I thought I had a real treasure. It was heavy and obviously very old. I thought I had a real find in my hands, but unfortunately it would not turn a profit. I paid thirty dollars and sold it for about the same. It was also much more expensive to mail than I originally assumed, and I got so frustrated trying to package it that I had a professional mailing service do it for me, which cost quite a bit. When all was said and done, I think I ended up losing about twenty bucks or so and really, more importantly, wasting quite a bit of valuable time. But I did learn a great lesson: not all big, old items will turn an acceptable profit. Some large, heavy items are worth quite a bit of money, but we are back to considering time management. If you do decide to purchase one of these types of items, it had better be at least somewhat valuable as most people will not pay a huge amount of postage for a lower-value item. (But they may pick it up from you; see section below regarding re-selling large and bulky items)

I have found that these types of bulky items are not worth the time, transportation, and extra space needed to store them. I once found some vintage motorboat engines. (Don't you love how that word "vintage" makes items sound so much more appealing?) I had every reason to believe each was probably worth $200 or more. I could have bought them for about $50 apiece, but they were so heavy I could barely even lift them. Clearly I would have turned a nice profit, but my selling them, ultimately, would not be worth the time or potential back injury.

Are there exceptions? Of course. For example, you may come across an antique sewing machine attached to a table. Such items can be worth a lot if they're the right ones. Right ones? How do you know that? In this case a sewing machine still attached to the original table could be one of the more common types that a huge number of households had, *or* it could be one of the more rare models that collectors drool over. This is where fast and proper research on your smartphone should reveal the answer. I typically pass on larger items, unless I can net more than $400–$500; otherwise, I am willing to take the chance that I missed out on a great opportunity.

Reselling Large and Bulky Items
I do not like packaging and mailing large bulky items; it's time consuming and a real hassle. I'd rather utilize my time doing something else. Let's take for example a vintage musical keyboard with a bulky stand. Some of those are quite large and burdensome. In a case like this, if I knew the keyboard had decent value and I can get it for the right price, I will still buy it, but I will advertise it as a "local pick up item only." In other words anyone can bid on it, but I'm not mailing or personally delivering it. They will have to come to me to pick it up. Only do this if you are comfortable with someone coming to you or even meeting in a public place for that matter. This is a personal decision; if you are comfortable, this is a great way to make a few extra bucks that you would have otherwise left behind.

Keep Some of Your Finds for Investment
As I articulated in "Vintage 1970s–1980s Collectibles," many of your finds can be great investments. There is nothing wrong with keeping some of them for yourself, especially if it's something you personally enjoy. There is no rule that you have to sell everything you find.

Diversity and Education
One of the most enjoyable parts of garage sailing for me is diversity. No two Saturdays will ever be the same—this I guarantee you. Boredom will not be a part of your new hobby. As a matter of fact, I have truly been blessed with an education throughout my years of buying and selling antiques, vintage stuff, and collectibles. I've learned about history, I've learned how other people lived in different generations, and I've learned about value. But out of all these wonderful attributes of sailing, I treasure most the historical education I've had. I can actually hold in my hand something that helped define an era. I find that concept quite fascinating. I hope you, too, find some kind of fulfillment in this part of the many aspects of garage sailing.

An End-of-chapter Thought
You have absorbed quite a bit of information, and you may feel overwhelmed. Rest assured that the process gets easier with time. With just a fraction of experience under your belt, you will find that properly classifying objects is enjoyable and easy to learn. I will say for the benefit of the reader and the ego of the professional dealer that this book is not meant to make you an expert on collectibles or antiques. I have the utmost respect for those professions, and I am sincerely in awe at the skill necessary to recognize the value and historical attributes of varied items. That said, this chapter has been meant to give you, the reader, some very simple nuts and bolts with which to start building your new hobby. You mix the ingredients in any way you like.

You may find that in general you really enjoy the field of antiques, vintage stuff, collectibles, and the like. You may decide to take things a step further and become more experienced with certain particular genres. If you do, write and give me some tips!

For the rest of you who bought this book for the sole reason of having fun and making some extra money, know that you now have enough information to help you start recognizing antiques, vintage stuff, and collectibles at garage sales. Go out there, enjoy yourself, and take some chances. I have no doubt you will find many roses among all those old thorns!

6
Other Salable Items

Training Your Eye to Spot Salable Items

OUR LAST CHAPTER addressed antiques and collectibles. Although those items will be a part of your sailing hobby, they are in *no* way the only means of income for you. It is quite the opposite actually; much of your income aside from DVDs, CDs, and books is going to come from used and unused finds that are not antiques or collectibles. This chapter addresses those items. Understand that there is absolutely no end to what can be sold on the Internet. With millions of people out there shopping online, the odds of one or more of them wanting a particular item is huge (though the desire might sometimes be difficult for us to understand).

Here is an obvious question you should ask yourself: "What are these items I should be looking for, and at what point do I back off? I mean, why shouldn't I go to a garage sale and just buy everything there, put it online, and see if someone bites?" You could do that, but my strong suspicion is that your doing so would fail miserably.

It is not true that *everything* can sell online. The truth is that certain objects attract attention and that some go completely ignored. How do I know this? When you put an item up for sale on eBay for instance, you can see how many people have clicked on it. The number of views could be dozens or even hundreds; the number could also be just a few or even none. So I will put this to rest right now: not *everything* will sell on the Internet!

It is important that we look at some of the reasons people buy a particular item to begin with. There are basically two motivating factors.

A Need Exists

I enjoy golf. I need to have some of the accessories that go along with the game, such as golf balls, tees, and gloves. I have no choice in the matter—I *must* have these items to play the game. I often purchase the necessities online because I can buy them at much lower prices and never have to leave my home. Comparison shopping is unnecessary because I already know what golf balls I like, what sort of tees I need, and what brand and size of golf gloves to purchase. I am simply doing my shopping online.

Look at your own shopping habits. When you go to the grocery store, for the most part, you know which brands you like and are comfortable with. Sure, every now and again, you do some comparison shopping, but for the most part, you go up and down the aisles, tossing your regular items into your basket; there is very little thought or decision making necessary. Buying online is no different. As a matter of fact, many buyers simply go to the same online seller to purchase certain things, just as you would go to the same store.

A Desire Exists

What is the difference between need and desire? I need to wear shoes, but I desire to have a particular designer pair of shoes. I need to eat to sustain myself, but I desire to eat certain types of food, some of which are not good for me. Many online buyers are making purchases based on desire rather than need. Perhaps they desire what they cannot afford in regular stores.

I remember years ago I really wanted a certain brand of watch. It was not outlandishly expensive but certainly beyond my budget at the time and, most importantly, very low on my priority list; there were many other necessities I needed to buy. I kept an eye on eBay and although it took a while, eventually one of these watches popped up for sale. It was brand new and still in the box, and the seller was reputable and asking for 75 percent below retail. I jumped on the deal and still, to this day, have and enjoy that watch. My point is that even though I certainly did not need it, I desired it, and at the right price, there would be no question that I would buy it. Many of your buyers will be in the same position. You will have something that means nothing to you but a great deal to them.

These are the main motivating factors behind someone making a purchase. If you break the factors down, they can go in a million different directions. Some desires are very close to needs or the other way around. Over time, you will begin to recognize certain items that you have reason to believe will be of some need or desire to other people.

But How Do I Know If It's Junk or Not?
You really don't. As the old saying goes, one person's junk is another's treasure.

You can, however, eliminate the odds of picking out items that will be big losers on the Internet. And remember that we are not referencing antiques, vintage stuff, and collectibles but newer items. Newer items are those that are not old enough to be antique or vintage. They are not the type of item that would typically be collected. They are items that have some usefulness in daily life. They could be tools, household items, office products, small kitchen appliances, bar accessories, crafts, sports-related items and the list goes on. Just think of the things you use or just enjoy having in your daily life. The problem is that there are so many varied items out there that it just makes no sense to buy them all; you would have to turn your home into a warehouse. As I mentioned, many items at garage sales have little to no salability. The following sections cover important factors to keep in mind as you peruse other people's "junk."

Profit
This topic is subjective because each one of us is different when it comes to what the minimum profit is that we will accept for our time and effort. Over time, you will start to figure out how long it takes you to research, list, maintain, sell, package, and mail an item. Such chores sound like a lot of hassle, but as you will learn in chapter 11, "Time Management," you can complete them relatively fast. But why bother at all if a low or even zero return is inevitable? For the most part, I will avoid taking the time to sell smaller items for less than ten dollars, medium-size items for less than twenty dollars, and larger items for less than fifty dollars. These figures are net after I've deducted the price of the item and all the related selling costs. Of course, the larger the item, the more time it takes to package, and the more room it takes up in my office; thus, I expect a bigger profit. This is a general guideline that I use to keep me from spending too much time for too little money. This rule typically doesn't apply to antiques, vintage stuff, and collectibles because those items sometimes sell for much more than I might have expected, so they are worth the risks. DVDs, CDs, and books are also an exception, as you will see in chapters 7 and 8.

Unused Items
There are lots out there! People buy things all the time and never use them. Often they were given as gifts and were never given a second thought after the gift wrap was taken off. Whatever the case, someone's unused item can be a very profitable find for you.

Packaged Items
Any item in its original packaging should demand your attention. If you find something, anything, that is in its original packaging, you should

consider buying it if the profit margin makes sense. Buyers obviously prefer unused items to used ones. For instance, you may find an unused five- or ten-year-old item that is no longer available on the open market. In other words, this particular object is relatively tough to find. Why? Well, obviously it was not a popular seller; otherwise, the same item would be for sale everywhere. However, there are still individuals out there who liked or used that particular item, and now they can't find it that easily. Here you have a winner. It's not a collectible, but neither is it a new item. These are products that some people have found useful. You have it, and certain people want it—a winning find for you and them.

This does not mean you should buy every packaged item you find. Here is where your common sense (and smartphone) will benefit you. If the item can be found elsewhere for a very low price, skip buying it. Let's say you found a box of a dozen newer average priced pens that has never been opened. Pens are very cheap, and you can easily find them in stores. They are simply not worth your attention. But let's say you found a case of boxes of pens. In that find, you may have potential. Someone who perhaps has a company that goes through lots and lots of pens might buy the lot, and you would make a healthy profit (depending on how much you paid for it).

Now let's say you found a football or a baseball bat that is boxed or sealed. Finding a case of them is unnecessary to make this purchase worthwhile. Of course, you can find them at any sporting-goods store, but for the most part, they're not cheap. In some cases, depending on brand and quality, they are quite expensive. Here you have an opportunity to make an average or substantial profit, depending on the quality of the item. The bottom line is that you have to use your own life experiences and common sense to make decisions on what kind of unopened, unused items to buy.

Unpackaged Items That Seem to Have Never Been Used
You will want to use the same frame of thought as you do when purchasing packaged items. The only difference is that you will need to

be much more selective. You should only purchase the kinds of items that you know are not inexpensive or easy to find; otherwise, you will be wasting your time. Buyers love packaging! In their minds, they feel as though they are getting a great deal because they are buying something identical to what they would buy in the store, and they are often right, so again, if you are buying an unpackaged item it had at least better be somewhat desirable.

Here are some of the drawbacks to people bidding on unpackaged items. In general, unpackaged items do not come with directions. A buyer may feel an unpackaged item might be broken since there is no box to protect it. You are also completely eliminating gift-giving buyers. Most people do not want to give or for that matter receive an unpackaged item as a gift.

Used Items

You will note a common theme throughout this book, and that is experience. I can give you advice that will enable you to save hours of frustration, time, and money, but the bottom line is that your own experience is going to help you more than anything. This rings equally true in regard to purchasing used and unpackaged items. Over time, it will become easier to determine the value in these types of products, but the following sections provide suggestions that will help put you on the right path.

Electronics

Examples would be electric drills or similar tools, radios, auto equipment, small appliances, cameras, and computer equipment. Be very careful here because it is not that easy for you to test such products right there at the garage sales. Occasionally, if it's just one rather expensive item you might want to have it tested, but for the most part it is just not time efficient or realistic to test everything. With other products, you can look at them and pretty much determine their condition—not so with electronic equipment. Even if an electronic item does work, potential buyers are still going to be leery about purchasing it. You may advertise that it works, but even if they do buy it, how do either of you know how long it's going to last? I rarely purchase electrical equipment unless it is boxed, never used, or has collectability potential. If, however, you decide to buy similar items, only purchase those that you know have quite a bit of value and that you can get at very low prices. For instance, if you know a certain electronic item you find would sell new for about one hundred dollars or more, go ahead and pick it up for a few bucks. Now you have an opportunity to resell it for about twenty-five to fifty dollars or more for a nice profit. Finally, always ask the sellers if such items work. They will usually tell you, and you can then honestly advertise that the person you had acquired the item from said it works. That coupled with you offering a money-back guarantee should help make buyers comfortable enough to bid.

Nonelectrical Household Items
These would be items like small hand tools, office products, households, and so forth. Items like these have a small return for the time involved in dealing with them. Again, use your common sense. If you see an item like this that you know is relatively expensive if purchased brand new, and if you can pick it up for a low price, go for it. Otherwise, avoid spending too much time on these types of products. Millions of them are out there.

Kitchenware
Now I am not referring to the antique and vintage collectible type we discussed in chapter 5, rather average ordinary kitchenware. These are items like plates, utensils, small appliances, barware, and glasses. In the context of these items, experience is absolutely vital. There is so much of this kind of stuff out there. Very few garage sales will be without some kind of kitchen item. Most are average, worthless dishware or utensils; however, sometimes you may come across

high-quality products. This is a different story. My recommendation is to talk to people who are familiar with this type of higher-end product and get their opinions. In addition, take a stroll through a high-end department store's housewares section and take notes. That's hands-on research and more direct. Of course you can also check higher-end products online and print them out. Just avoid spending and exaggerated amount of time milling through all that stuff looking for some kind of treasure. Time when sailing is crucial. Use your best judgment.

Miscellaneous

This would be everything else imaginable! All I can tell you is to use everything you've learned in this book and combine it with your own experience and with that little voice in your head. You will find that this combination can accurately discern the valuable items in the vast array of miscellaneous products.

Perhaps some people are out only looking for the big wins. I think such tunnel vision is unwise. They are eliminating the opportunity to make a tidy profit with many types of items. Although buying and selling antiques and collectibles may be more profitable and quite honestly much more fun, don't overlook the level of profit in items that are not antiques or collectibles.

7

DVDs and CDs, Your Bread and Butter

NEXT TO ANTIQUE and collectible items, DVDs and CDs are one of my favorite avenues of profit. I call them the bread and butter of the business because they're dependable and steady. The profits are sometimes small but consistently healthy, perhaps not as healthy as a rare phonograph or antique model ship, but all the smaller profits quickly add up. In the context of DVDs and CDs, you have two things going for you. First, they are quite easy to find at garage sales and can be purchased at extremely low prices. Second, there are lots and lots of buyers on the Internet looking for them. In other words, the supply *and* demand are both quite high, an extremely rare combination! I have put together three systems for liquidating DVDs and CDs. The first emphasizes the individual sale of each one, while the second is selling in bulk, which is quicker but not as profitable an avenue. The other—the one I favor—is selling on Amazon, which I referenced in chapter 1, in the section titled "Setting Up Your Internet Account." I prefer using Amazon because my time is limited. There is no right or wrong way to sell these items. I advise that you look at (and try) all systems and use the one that works best with your schedule and pocketbook. But before we get into the specifics of each system, let's look at what is out there and what you should and should not purchase.

DVDs
They're easily found and for a good reason: unlike music CDs, which people listen to over and over again, people generally watch individual DVDs only once or twice if at all. The good thing is that because of that, they are usually in very good shape or perhaps never even opened. With the onslaught of Blu-ray, you should be seeing even more regular DVDs out there.

What Kind of DVDs Am I Buying?
Following is a list of some of the genres you will find with my suggestions. But first a footnote; unlike CDs you will most likely not be buying DVDs in large bulk purchases unless it's appropriate. Collections of DVDs mostly contain unsalable very common blockbuster releases.

Drama and Comedy DVDs
These are very common and the bulk of what you will find. Over time, you will learn to distinguish which ones have value and which are worthless. For the most part, however, if a DVD cover shows a recognizable movie with recognizable actors, it's probably quite common. Unless the seller is practically giving such DVDs away, I would avoid buying them. On the flip side, if I see a movie that has actors or movies I don't recognize then I will buy it but for no more than a buck apiece, less if possible especially if I'm buying a few of them. If the movie is a classic older movie, I will always buy it. I will say, however, that you will probably find some movies that you do not recognize and/or are classic but are all but worthless. If after you have gotten home you run across some of these, look on the back for the manufacturer's name; if over time you see that same manufacturer seems to have a lot of worthless movies, then it's a safe bet to stay away from buying anything with their name on it.

Children's DVDs

You will see quite a few of these. Kids have a tendency of growing up, and when that happens, the parents are caught with an abundance of children's unused things, including DVDs. Be careful, though. Unlike most adults, kids tend to watch the same movie over and over again. If what you're about to buy looks rather beat up or, yes, even chewed, you might want to skip it. In addition, you will find that children's DVDs are found in bulk. The parents may have dozens that they are trying to ditch. Get a bulk amount cheap enough, and the few damaged ones you find within the mix won't hurt so much. If I cannot get a good deal in bulk or it's just not a bulk purchase, I will typically pay no more than fifty cents per DVD, a buck if they're sealed. Also children DVDs tend to do well being resold in bulk. A newer parent can save quite a bit of money not buying brand new individual DVDs that will get outgrown in no time. The sealed DVDs, however, or some of the more rare ones can be sold individually.

Exercise DVDs

These are hit and miss. With time and experience, you will learn to recognize the more common exercise DVDs from the rarer ones. There are some exercise gurus out there who are quite famous. You are probably not going to get much. But if you find an exercise DVD about how to exercise to hula music or belly dancing music, you may have a winner! Exercise DVDs do well when sold in bulk, so buy them but at a good price, such as twenty-five to fifty cents each. If they look obscure or are still sealed, pay a buck each but no more. Those might sell well individually.

Instructional DVDs

I am referencing DVDs that in general are related to things like sports such as golf, tennis, or fishing. You may also find instructions on everything from car repair to carpentry. These can sell extremely well, because they typically have a shorter production run. If you find something like dog-training DVDs, you probably have a real winner! Pay as little as you can and no more than two dollars per DVD, unless you see one you've sold before for a great price, then pay whatever you need to. But it's not that common for a seller to ask for more than one or two dollars each, especially later in the day. I would say the most common price is a dollar. These you will most likely not be selling in bulk but rather selling individually.

Educational DVDs

Examples of educational videos would be about nature, history, biography, or politics. Just like instructional DVDs, these can be very hot sellers. Buy them all. Don't hesitate to pay a dollar, but of course try to get it lower if you're buying multiple copies. Same as instructional DVDs, these will most likely be sold individually.

Self-Help and Psychology DVDs

You may find some of these in sets—in other words, a boxed set of multiple DVDs. Just about everyone wants to better their lives. Buy these. They'll almost always sell very well individually. Since these mostly come in multiple discs, I'll go up to maybe two or three bucks. You may even want to watch them for yourself first!

DVD Sets

You will also find some DVDs in large sets. They may be either fiction or nonfiction. In general, they are good buys. They can be great finds because not that many of them were made. Your finding every episode of some old TV series could mean a set of a dozen or so discs. Make every effort to buy these sets because they usually sell extremely well as do British Broadcasting Company (BBC) sets.

But if a set comprises a recent miniseries or TV series, skip it unless you can pick it up for a buck. Such sets were likely mass produced. People bought them, but they lost popularity as fast as they became famous. Conversely, if you find a TV series from the sixties through the nineties, you probably have a winner. I'll pay up to five dollars if I know or even have a suspicion the series has potential as described above.

Multidisc DVDs
Now this is different than DVD sets. These are DVDs that have multidiscs in one case as opposed to the sets that typically have multicases in one collection. If you find a DVD with more than one disc *and* you do not recognize it as a blockbuster movie then pick it up; even for two bucks, it might be a good find.

Video Games
In general, sellers set high prices for newer games. Just skip them. What we are seeing now is a resurgence in games like the old Nintendo and Ataris that we referred to in chapter 5. Even the early Playstation games can do well. Some older folks want to relive that part of their childhood, and such games are big sellers. Some are even quite collectible and have lots of value. Some will sell quite well individually, if not then accumulate a few dozen or so and then sell them in bulk. I'll typically pay no more than a dollar a game.

Four Types of DVDs to Stay Away From
DVDs with Missing Covers
You will find an abundance of these. Even if you think it's a rare movie, just pass on it. You need the cover.

DVDs Marked "For Promotional Purposes Only" or "For Your Consideration"
Phrases like these means that it may be unallowable to sell. They were given to viewers for things like promotional or rating purposes. Do not buy these kind of DVDs.

Sports DVDs
These are different than instructional. These are typically clips of famous sports plays, Super Bowl highlights, that kind of thing. Stay away from them. They are typically terrible sellers. Unfortunately if you are buying in bulk, you may have no other choice than to include these.

Copied DVDs
They are obviously copied and not from the appropriate manufacturer. Don't buy them.

Collectible VHS
I added this section under DVDs because not long ago VHS was still utilized by many people; obviously that has changed, but now we are finding that some VHS are coming into their own as being collectible. Horror seems to be the biggest seller, and the cheesiest and most *unknown* horror flicks are the best finds. When you have nothing else to do or when you're watching TV, just start searching the Internet or eBay for sold VHS tapes, from the highest to the lowest. Doing so will give you a feel for what you need to be looking for. Remember: always check the end of the auction sold items only, not active auctions.

Sometimes you have no choice but to buy certain items in bulk, and that is especially pertinent to buying VHS tapes. Some sellers have multiple boxes of them and want them *all* gone, not just a few tapes. The sellers may offer them for fifty cents apiece or five or ten bucks for a hundred or so of them, but the sellers will probably tell you that you have to take them all! In these cases, they are trying to save themselves the time and effort of hauling them away. If you see treasures amid the junk, go ahead and gladly accept their offer.

CDs
For the most part CDs will not be as abundant as DVDs. People are more apt to keep their CDs and listen to them over and over again

unlike movies. However, with the onslaught of easy downloading, CDs have been more prevalent at garage sales.

What Kind of CDs Am I Buying?

Rock 'n' Roll, Rap, and Hip-Hop

These can be a winner. Music from artists such as the Rolling Stones or Led Zeppelin can sell very well. Some of the common names in rock have kept their popularity and can still be resold. The same goes with Rap and Hip-Hop. But be careful, again popularity and an abundance of merchandising typically go hand in hand. With time you will be able to discern value for this type of genre. I have, however, discovered CDs of many other artists of these genres that I have never even heard of that have sold for a bundle. If you have never heard of the artist, buy the CD!

Classical, New Age, Blues and Jazz

A decent amount of demand exists for this type of music, and relevant CDs can be worth quite a bit. If you see them, buy them. You will also see a lot of classical music CDs that have never been opened—a huge plus!

Country and Comedy

They could be problematic. For the most part, they do not do well for resale; however, if I see anything from the 1950s–1960s, I would buy it. Some of those old timers have a very good following, or they're so obscure that the supply is low enough to make this a potentially good win for you.

Teen, Country, Generic, and Holiday Music

You are going to find many, many modern teen CDs as well as loads of holiday and generic type music. What I mean by generic is that there is no artist mentioned; it's just a collection of songs or instrumentals. Now I am not advising you not to buy these, but don't make a special effort to do so. If they're in a lot of other CDs you're buying in bulk then take them, there's still some possible value there. Some seasonal CDs can be sold individually, but for the most part you'll be bulk selling them as one big collection right before the holidays are about to come upon us. Same as the other genres; you can typically get something for them in bulk. If not there are other methods of liquidating them as we will discuss toward the end of this chapter.

Self-Help CDs
They usually come in sets of multiple discs; buy these!

Audio Books on CD
These can do very, very well. We are crossing over a bit with books as you will see in the rest of the chapter. As with self-help CDs, these usually come in sets of multiple discs, so go ahead and buy.

Everything Else
You are going to come across all sorts of music that is tough to put into a category, partly because it's so obscure but often because you simply do not recognize it. These can be great finds, so grab all you see.

Four Types of CDs to Stay Away From
CDs without the Case or Inserts
You'll find plenty of these. Avoid them. Just as with DVDs, they are simply not worth buying. Also, some will be in their cases but without the front or back covers or both (these covers are called inserts or the artwork). Avoid the ones missing any of the covers.

CDs Marked "For Promotional Purposes Only"
Such CDs were probably given to listeners for promotional or rating purposes. Do not purchase.

Copied CDs
They are obviously copied and not from the appropriate manufacturer. Don't buy them.

CD Singles
These are CDs with just a few songs on them. They could be likened to the old forty-five records, where you would get two of the more popular songs instead of having to purchase the entire album. Stay away from CD singles; they are poor sellers. Unfortunately, if you are buying everything at one price, you may have no other choice but to include these. I put them aside in a box marked singles, and then when I get one hundred or so, I sell them in bulk.

How Much Do I Pay?

Bulk (The Good, the Bad, and the Ugly)
Your best scenario is to always try to buy in bulk. As far as pricing is concerned, nothing is set in concrete; you must get to know the collection and make your offer based on what you feel the value is. Whenever buying bulk have a top price in mind and start low but not so low you risk insulting the seller. For example if I saw a box of about two hundred CDs and noticed a good 50 to 75 percent were potential winners, then I would probably start with forty dollars. I try to keep the twenty-five-cent-per-CD calculation in my head, and then I start a little lower than that. Would I go to fifty cents each (in other words one hundred dollars)? Probably not, unless the percentage of winners were high enough. Otherwise I would probably go to maybe sixty dollars for this bulk purchase.

Bulk (Lots and Lots of CDs But Too Many Bad and Ugly)
If you are buying in bulk but see lots of losers, then before you even make the deal separate the ones you want from the bad ones if it's appropriate and won't take you too long. When you approach the seller, simply make a bulk offer on what you have separated from the rest of the collection.

Individual CDs

If there are only a handful of CDs, then I would pay up to one dollar each if they are in very good condition and if I do not recognize the artist. The only real exceptions are the ones I know have good value and/or the ones that are still sealed. I rarely pay more than a buck for any CD.

But again that's if there is literally just a handful to choose from. If there are more, I will try a mini bulk deal. Let's say for example they wanted a dollar apiece and I found eight worth buying, I would offer five bucks.

Individual Artist with Multiple Discs

In other words two or more disc sets (they typically are not more than three discs). I definitely pay a dollar. I'll even go to two dollars. These can often be very good sellers.

Bulk (But the Seller Is Just Not on Board)

Now let's say you do have a bulk lot to make an offer on, but this seller is simply not going with the program. In this instance I would treat it just like buying the individual CDs, but the only difference is since I'm probably going to buy a lot of them (but not the entire collection), I will still try for a lower price. If that doesn't work and I've been careful about choosing quality, I'll pay the seller the respective amount; this is as articulated above for individual CD purchases.

Self-Help and Audio Books

I would pay up to three dollars if they are in nice condition. If it's a huge set, I will go up to about five bucks, unless I know from past experience I have a winner, then I will pay accordingly.

Collectible Music: Eight-Tracks and Cassettes
Tape Cassettes

You will most probably find dozens or more tape cassettes on Saturdays. Pay no attention to any that do not have a case and the inserts. For the ones that do, you are still going to need to be very selective. My advice is to stay away from them, except for classic rock from the sixties and seventies. Many of these have value as collectors' items. In addition, buy any rap or hip-hop. Much of that music was coming out right around the time things were shifting to CDs, which is why I think some are collectible. When doing your at-home smartphone searches in your spare time, include cassettes. This will help you discover other genres or artists outside classic rock and rap that have collectible value. For all intents and purposes, cassettes are practically free. I would not pay more than twenty-five to fifty cents each. If you come across a few dozen, you can probably get them all for five bucks. The only exception might be the rap and hip-hop cassettes. I may pay as much as a buck apiece for those, but it's rare that I'm ever charged that much.

Eight-Track Tapes
These old dinosaurs from the seventies are nostalgic to look at, but that's about it. Very few people use them. What you want to look for is collectability. Some of these eight-tracks have become highly collectible. I would lean mostly toward rock 'n' roll, but buy them all and go through them later; remember, you should be getting these for a song anyway. I would urge you to stay away from more of the mellow type of rock or country; you might get lucky, but again we want to put the odds in our favor. Just like with cassettes, eight-tracks are the perfect example of scrolling down eBay auctions while lying around the house; you would be surprised what is in demand. Finally, if you find any eight-track carrying cases, pay a couple bucks more. A lot of buyers want them for nostalgic reasons or to hold their collection.

Format to Selling DVDs and CDs
I have my own personal system. You can use it or tweak it around your own needs. Here's the system I have found to be the most productive, profitable, and time efficient.

Amazon (Reread Chapter 1, Section "Why I Use Amazon")
Always read Amazon's rules and guidelines and keep up with the changes; that said, become an Amazon seller. It's easy to join, just like eBay. You can sell just about anything on Amazon, but for the purposes of this section, we are going to refer to DVDs and CDs. But here's a disclaimer: as of this writing, Amazon has put some restrictions on DVD sales. So although some people do qualify to sell DVDs on Amazon, it's a little more complicated and problematic than selling CDs. For now, we are only going to refer to CDs.

Check Amazon to see if you can or wish to become a DVD seller and if it's for you. If so then read their rules and then proceed to list If you are not going to sell DVDs on Amazon or some of the DVDs you have to list do not have value then liquidate those DVDs in the same way CDs are liquidated as recommended in this section.

Selling Merchant Fulfilled Network (MFN)
If you choose to sell through MFN, you will need to look at what the non-Prime prices are and see if your CDs are worth listing. There is no right or wrong answer. Again, I do not sell through MFN, but if I did, I would want to net at least five bucks per CD plus shipping, to make the selling worth my time.

Selling Fulfilled by Amazon (FBA)
In my opinion, FBA is the only way to go. Once you have listed and shipped the relevant items to Amazon, you're done. Aside from inconsequential things like checking your competition and changing the prices, you do virtually nothing but wait for the money to show up in your bank account. I mean *nothing*. You don't do shipping. You don't deal with the buyer. You don't deal with returns. You don't deal with packaging items—nothing! We are going to move forward in this section as if you are selling FBA.

Enter Barcode or Title into Amazon's Seller System
Type in the barcode on the CD (or you can buy an inexpensive scanner that reads barcodes for you). You'll know it (the barcode) when you see it. If there is no number then just type in the title of the CD. Once you type or scan (do consider buying that scanner; they're so easy and inexpensive and will save you so much time!) that item will usually pop up.

Check the Lowest Offer Price with Your Same Condition
Since you are selling FBA, check "Prime Members Only" prices in your search. When you see what the Prime members are being offered for that certain CD in similar condition, check that price and see if it's within your comfort zone. If it is then list it! I must add, however, that everyone's comfort level could be different. For me personally I would want to net at least five dollars per CD after all costs to make the process worth it. However, if I have already gone through the process of scanning and checking and I see that I will only net about two or three bucks, I'll probably still do it. Why? Because I have already gone this far in the process so what the heck. That said if I knew beforehand that I would net that little I simply would not move forward in the process. The amazing thing is that many of the CDs I find will sell in a higher range—well into the ten- to twenty-dollar-plus range—all for an investment of typically fifty cents or less.

Amazons Tools
Among other tools, Amazon has a wonderful feature wherein you put your item title or barcode in and it will break down the cost for you so you will know before you list it about how much you are going to make. After a while you will get to know the type items that will yield a decent enough profit and not have to check each and every time.

Tough-Selling CDs

Amazon will let you know if your item is going to be a tough sale prior to you completing the listing. I figure they know what they're talking about, so I almost always adhere to their advice and do not proceed with the listing.

Condition

Once you have decided that you are going to sell a CD on Amazon, check its condition. That way you know how to list them. I always sell my CDs in very good to like-new condition, or brand new if I got lucky. Amazon has a reference to describing a CD's condition; read these and even print them out and have them somewhere accessible so you can easily refer to them. If they do not meet the very good-like-new condition guidelines, I will only sell them if they are relatively high-priced CDs, and I always describe their defects; otherwise, I will not sell a CD that is not at least in very good condition. Once you've finished listing all the pertinent CDs, just follow Amazon's instructions, ship them, and for all intents and purposes you are done!

Online Sites That Will Buy Your Unwanted CDs

If you find your CD is worth less than your effort of selling it on Amazon or if the condition does not meet your standards then set it aside in a box labeled "check online." I usually wait until I have a couple hundred or so CDs. There are online CD companies that will buy your CDs (they will also buy your DVDs). You do the same thing you did when researching on Amazon. Type in or scan the barcode, and see what they are offering. After you type or scan, the offers comes up immediately; there is no waiting. If an offer is twenty-five cents or more, I just sell as long as the company is paying the postage. Condition really does not matter with these, unless you can determine that it is definitely not what their condition restrictions demand. However, often it's difficult to tell so if that's the case send it in and let the company decide if they want to buy it or not.

Sell on eBay

Here is where you get those online companies to help you. If you put in a barcode and suddenly a large number pops up—that is, a few bucks or more—then you know you have something of value, even though it was not a good Amazon seller. Somehow there is still value. Take that CD and check on eBay to see how much it can sell for. You'll be surprised. Sometimes the amount is a tidy sum. If the CD is in very good to like-new condition, list it on eBay. Just find your comfort zone for the minimum you would take. The amount for me? If I can net five dollars or more over what the Internet site was offering me, I'll probably stick the CD on eBay and ship it myself. Now put that CD in a box labeled "sell on eBay." Keep in mind five dollars does not sound like a lot but all these sales add up, you would be surprised.

Unwanted CDs Sold by Genre

If the Internet company does not want your CDs or offers you less than the respective twenty-five to fifty cents per CD, then I suggest you separate them by genre. If you have a bunch of classical CDs, put them aside. If you have a bunch of meditation CDs, put them aside as well. If you see a number of CDs by the same artist, put them aside too.

Now check the condition of the CDs. If they are in very good to like-new condition, put those in a separate box marked "sell by genre." Once you have a hundred or so of any particular genre then you can bulk sell them. You will most likely get more money than you think, because buyers often want to buy CDs from their favorite genres or artists in bulk to build their collections and save themselves not only a lot of hassle but also from having to buy individual CDs and pay all those shipping costs. Remember that individually these CDs are all but worthless, but in a group, they have value. Separate by genre and you will have made a nice profit. One side note, if you see a number of CDs by the same artist and if they are in very good or better condition, I would urge you to try to sell these as one lot before you even check what the online company will pay you. If they don't sell as one lot, then go ahead and offer them to the Internet company.

Loser CDs
Take the rest of the CDs that are either not in good condition, don't fit into any genre, or for whatever reason are unsalable and put them in a standard file box—the kind I told you to buy in ten packs. They will hold about 175 CDs or so. When you have about half dozen boxes (around one thousand CDs), advertise them for a cheap price. I typically use Craigslist. I would ask $200 and settle for $100 just to get rid of them. For anything less than that, I am better off taking the CDs to a donation center—or better yet having them picked up directly from me to save myself the work. I might add, however, that selling on Craigslist can be a hassle, and quite frankly having strangers come to your home or place of business can be a bit unsettling. Even meeting them at a public place is uncomfortable. It is also a bit labor intensive lugging boxes of CDs around. You just need to make your own choice on that avenue of selling.

Just be upfront when advertising on Craigslist or what have you, but don't go into too much detail. If they start asking you questions about where you got them and so on, just tell them the truth, but keep it simple. Just say you've been getting these from garage and estate sales over the past year or so, they are in varied conditions and you decided to not keep them. Tell them the collection was taking up room and you need it out ASAP. Take lots of close-up photos so the buyers can see the titles; this way you do not have to manually write each title into your description, same as when you sell genre lots of CDs in bulk on eBay. Make sure you let potential buyers know that they can have fifteen minutes to look them over and that they cannot "cherry-pick," a term referring to a situation where people will only take the CDs that have some value. Remember that some online sellers sell CDs individually but for a very, very low price; they are making their money in different ways. They're not making a lot per sale, but they do lots and lots and lots of sales, so they'll be glad to take these off your hands.

Selling CDs Individually in Quantity

Hey! Perhaps you would like to be one of those sellers who make small profits on quantity sales. If so look into it, and if it's for you, then just keep the CDs for yourself. I personally don't have the time or patience to make money this way. If I did, my fun hobby would turn into more of a larger, time-demanding business and take me away from other things I want or have to do, but perhaps in your case this might be perfect! If it's DVDs you might wish to sell in this fashion then again, as stated above see Amazon for their rules and restrictions with regard to selling DVDs.

So there it is, an assembly line of sorts to extract as much profit from your CDs as possible.

Media Mail

The USPS has what is called media mail; this is an extremely inexpensive way to sell items such as CDs and DVDs and books. I often take advantage of this service. If for example I am only selling one CD or DVD, I'll typically send it first class, but for the bulkier or multiple CD, DVD or book packages, I will always use media mail. Check with the USPS about rules mailing in this way. Of course always check other mailing houses and use the service that works best for you and your pocket book.

8

Books, More Than Your Bread and Butter: Also Your Dessert!

I HAVE A feeling some of you are going to only want to do this! It can be a goldmine. We are so fortunate to have Amazon, not just for books and CDs but for all sorts of things. Amazon has always been a huge magnet for book buyers. Books can be one of the more exciting aspects of sailing. Not only is buying general books to sell on Amazon lucrative, but while sailing we also have a much higher probability of discovering collectible finds. Books are abundant. Please note however, as of this writing Amazon has certain restrictions, so approval is needed to sell collectible books .When discussing selling books on Amazon we will be referring to general non-collectible books only. We will however still address collectible books and the best way to handle that avenue of revenue.

The printing press was invented by the Roman Empire in the mid-fifteenth century, although some would argue that the Chinese invented printing centuries before then. But let's go with the European invention of the press. (Hang tight, I *am* going somewhere with this!) Now, right around 1900, the vinyl record was invented (technically records were originally made of shellac not vinyl; who knows maybe that little bit of information will come in handy one day while sailing!)

An any rate that gives books about a 450-year head start! What was needed with the vinyl? A costly phonograph. But for books? Only a pair of eyes was needed! Although it's highly unlikely you will be coming across books more than 125 or so years old, my point is that books have played a huge part in the fabric of our society for centuries, and there are lots and lots (did I say *lots*?) of them out there!

Yes, today we have e-books, but that does not take away from the fact that the written word on paper will always be in demand. A vast amount of people prefer to hold a book. They enjoy the endearing warmth and feel of actual books as opposed to the coldness of electronic devices. Face it—printed books are not going anywhere.

With so many books, what does one do after driving up to a garage sale to find multiple boxes stacked with the printed word? Sure, a book dealer can take one glance and know value, but how can the rest of us? What I have learned from years of practice you get to learn in about thirty minutes. I've dealt with bookstores. I've asked lots of questions. I've explored eBay and Amazon and what sells the best. I've done hours of research, and here are some simple facts. If you want to delve into the art and business of collecting books, the information is there for you to study and explore. But if you just want a basic working knowledge to get in and out of a garage sale quickly while carrying stacks of value in your arms, then read on.

Old Does Not Always Mean Valuable
Just because a book is old does not mean it's valuable. It took me years to figure this one out. I used to pick up an old book, open it up, and glance at the copyright. Wow, I would think, printed at the turn of the century, well more than one hundred years old! I'd better grab this and any others I find fast before someone else sees them.

But a book's age doesn't always determine its value. Yes, an older book can be a real treasure, but you and I are not experts at this. What's more, you will not have the time to pick up a handful of old books at garage sales and cross-reference them on your smartphone like you would with individual items. So what do you do? You have choices. If you choose to start perusing these books, you should first look at their titles and authors. If you recognize a title or author even if it's not a first edition, grab the book; now remember I am referring to very old books. If you do not recognize the title or author then turn to the first few pages and look for the copyright. If you see first edition or just one year printed, you may have a first edition (or perhaps not; see the appendix for reference information on first editions).

Now you have a decision to make: take it or leave it. Personally, unless I recognize the author or title I would probably leave it. I've bought many old books with authors and titles I've never heard of, even first editions, that turned out to have little value. That does not mean you shouldn't buy them, but if you do I would not pay more than a buck apiece or cheaper if you can bundle them up. Have a special box in your car and safely place them in there. When you have time, you can cross-reference them online for value. It's a little like playing a slot machine. You may have something worth exactly what you paid, a buck, or you may have a nice ten-to-twenty-dollar book. If your luck is good, you may have a fifty-to-one-hundred-dollar book. Getting anything worth more means you're on a hot machine! So it comes down to you not minding hauling these things around (books are heavy) and taking a few hours out of your day to play the book slots. There is no right or wrong answer.

Classic Authors and Titles
I'm not talking about authors from one hundred plus years ago, but relatively modern twentieth-century writers, such as Hemmingway, Steinbeck, Capote, and so forth. This is yet another example where kicking back and watching TV with your smartphone comes in handy. During a commercial or boring part of your show, just start searching for famous authors' names from, say, about forty-plus years ago. You will recognize a lot of names, but you will also see many you will never have heard of, who may still actually be quite famous in modern

culture. Just keep trying to store those names in the back of your mind or write them down. Eventually, you will be at a sale, and there one of the names will pop up. One of the authors you researched will be staring you right in the face. It's exciting. Pick up the relevant book, turn to the first few pages, and check out the copyright. If it even looks like it could be a first edition, grab it. Otherwise, I'd let it go. Be on guard, however, for "Book of the Month" and Readers Digest editions; avoid those.

Modern Authors

More so than collectible or antique books, condition is key. These authors are more contemporary: Stephen King, Michael Crichton, Anne Rice, and so on. Too recent to be valuable? No, not at all, but be on your guard because there are simply many of their books out there. You'll find scores of a modern author's hardback and paperback books, trust me. The problem is that you need a first edition and, for the most part, an early first edition—in other words, one of the first few books written by that author before he or she became famous. The author at that time was not famous enough to mass produce, so finding a first edition can be a real find. Come across a first edition of *Carrie* by Stephen King, and you are holding about $2,000 in your hand. Also, some of these authors often did a lot of signings, especially when they were just starting out. Turn to the first few pages. If you see a signature, grab it, first edition or not. I have a beautiful copy of one of Anne Rice's books, signed by the author herself. I got it for about a buck and kept it. I still have it.

The real issue is that unlike the hundred-year-old books, there are going to be many more of these. You need to make a judgment call and decide for yourself how much time you want to spend on sifting through these books, but if you do, please stick with first edition books that have the dust jacket. But even first editions you find can be time consuming looking up but like with the old books, you can save them for a rainy day to see if any of the ones you found have good value. Not a lot of value in the first editions you find? That's okay you can sell them in bulk, you can also sell non-first editions in bulk. "Nice Lot of Twenty Hardback Stephen King Novels," for example. But again you have to decide just how much time you want to invest. You also have to look at the risk/reward factor.

Mass-Market Paperbacks

These are those smaller often kind of thick cheap-looking paperbacks you see everywhere including grocery stores, airport gift shops, and so forth. They are usually about four-by-seven inches. Skip them unless you see a whole bunch written by an author you have not heard of. He or she probably has a following. And since the writer is not that well known, there probably have not been huge numbers of his or her books printed, unlike famous authors, such as Danielle Steele or John Grisham. No matter if these books are from the sixties, seventies, or last year, if you see a group of them, buy the whole lot. Chances are you'll be able to sell for a nice profit. Yes, you can buy a grouping of books by famous author too, but you will be doing a lot of lifting and hard work for a relatively low profit.

Trade Paperbacks (Big Amazon Seller!)

Remember: condition is key. It doesn't have to be perfect, but stay away from beat- up books. We've already discussed the aforementioned mass-market books, which are cheaply made. Trade paperbacks typically show much more quality. Trade paperbacks are generally about eight-by-five inches or more, so they are larger than mass-market ones. They are often sold in bookstores and online and are typically more expensive than the mass-market ones. You will be buying many of these that you find, but mostly you will be concentrating on nonfiction. I'm not referring to books like the Complete Idiot's Guide series or Chicken Soup for the Soul books. I'm talking about things you don't come across all that often. I am referring to books from any nonfiction subject you can imagine: *Navajo Indian*

Weaving Styles or *Gem Cutting: A Lapidary's Manual.* That second title I paid a buck for and sold for twenty-five dollars. If you find a book about underwater diving off an obscure island in Greece to photograph a rare fish that only comes out in June but only when the moon is full, then definitely go for it! My point is that the more strange and obscure, the better.

These books, believe it or not, have a huge profit potential. Why?—there is not that much interest in them, right? Correct, there's not that much interest in them. But guess what? There was enough interest to publish it in the first place, which means low publication numbers along with some interest. Amazon is huge. Someone is looking for *The Stanley Plane: A History and Descriptive Inventory* and will pay well for the book. I sold that very book for forty-five dollars on Amazon. Yes, Amazon will take a share. But all I did was take a few minutes to list it and ship it to their warehouse with a bunch of other books I listed. And I only paid about a buck for the Stanley Plane book. So even though there is not a huge demand, the demand is enough for a nice profit.

How about religious books? They're nonfiction, right? Right, so buy them! Philosophy titles, history, human behavior, business, psychology, medicine, music, history—the list goes on. Is there anything in nonfiction to avoid? Of course there is. Although there still may be value, I typically stay away from any book with a highly recognized author or older perhaps outdated self-helps; many of them were massed produced and some of the older ones may no longer be relevant to a lot of people. Sometimes the book will tell you not to buy it. It might state something like "a million sold" or "Best seller." Recognize the name Oprah? Dr. Phil? Bill Clinton? If the name is big and very recognizable, then that typically means big production runs. Lots of supply and perhaps a fading demand.

Can you buy fiction trade paperbacks? Yes of course, but by buying nonfiction, I feel you are putting the odds more in your favor. Understand, nonfiction is easy to discern value by the subject matter;

fiction can be more hit and miss. Experiment, buy some fiction trade paperbacks (not mass market), and see what kind of price it demands on Amazon. Try to stick with titles and authors you do not recognize.

Nonfiction Hardbacks
Yes, same as trade paperbacks; buy them too but the dust jacket is a very important factor.

Oversized Hardbacks
Some of them are referred to as "coffee table books." If the subject matter is out of the ordinary, you could have a winner, but be careful, these books are heavy and cumbersome; experience alone should be your best teacher on these monsters.

Oversized Paperbacks
You could have something here. They are not "coffee table books" and are not as heavy. They are often about nonfiction subjects and may have great value. For example, I once found boxes of oversized paperbacks all about how to make jewelry. The seller wanted a buck apiece no matter how many I bought, which is quite the exception since sellers typically jump at offers for entire lots of books. I think in this case there was an emotional attachment to them. At any rate I still did a little bargaining. There were over fifty of them. I paid around forty dollars; that's a lot for an unsure bet of books at a garage sale. I won though; many sold for between ten and fifty dollars each. I pur-chase just about every oversized paperback I see unless I know from experience that it's worthless.

Textbooks
Now you could be talking some major money. Students are typically on a tight budget. Some textbooks sell new for well over $100—and quite often much, much more. But be careful: some can become

dated very fast. I once bought a huge box of nursing books for $10. Many sold for $25 to $50 each, but they were only a couple of years old, if that. But there're always exceptions, of course. Some of the more obscure textbooks, even if they're a few years old, can sell for an unimaginable amount of money. For instance, the tenth edition of *Introduction to General Organic and Biochemistry in the Laboratory* from 2011, not even in that great a shape, sold for over $1,000 about five years after that publication year. So keep your eye out; even the older ones can obviously do very well.

Cookbooks
Some are collectible, and yes, some do well on Amazon, but be extra careful with condition; remember many of these books were kept and used in kitchens, so the likelihood of them having stains is much higher.

Audio Books
As we saw in the CD section, audio books are a great find; pick everyone up you see.

Sets
Typically hardbacks sets consist mostly of nonfiction. For example, *Time Life* has a set of twenty-six leather-bound books about the Old West. They can fetch about $100 to perhaps $150 sometimes more depending on condition. You will usually end up paying about $25—a good profit. *Reader's Digest* and *National Geographic* also have sets of books, but be careful. Not all publishers like *Time Life*, *Reader's Digest*, or *National Geographic* sets have value. This is one of the few times when buying books that I would suggest using your smartphone to check before making an offer. Soft cover sets are out there too but might not demand the price for an acceptable profit but you never know. As with hardback sets check your smartphone.

Condition Is Key!

They do not have to be in pristine condition, but if they seem relatively worn, if their spines are loose, if their pages have creases or writing, or they smell moldy or mildewy, skip them. But in general do not spend too much time checking books out, you will immediately know by the look of the cover. You could start flipping through each one to make sure there is no writing etcetera, but that is very time consuming; just assume that if it looks good on the outside, it's fine on the inside. Will you discover that some are not so nice inside after you get home? Of course, but again, put the odds in your favor, and judge the book by the cover! You will save valuable time this way. Just as with CDs, most online sellers will have a guide on how to describe condition. You can also download an overview definition of each physical part of a book; it will help you better describe condition because you can more intelligently refer to the proper part of the book. Just print it out and put it next to your desk for easy access. The exceptions are older books mentioned in the sections above. Even there, condition is a key factor, but because of the age and potential value of certain books, they could be worth buying even if they're not in the best of condition.

A Few Basic Collectible Book-Scouting Hints

First Editions

Making sure a book is a first edition can be tricky at times, so make your scouting easy on yourself; take into consideration everything you have learned in this chapter thus far. If a book says first edition as mentioned earlier, buy it. If it does not but has only one year, buy it. If it says nothing, buy it anyway. Many times, publishers will make it easy for you. They will print which editions their books are or have a number of different years on them; sometimes they do both. In a case where a book has multiple years printed in its front matter, avoid buying it. Collectors love first editions. My advice is to take about an hour out of your schedule and get on a couple of book-collector websites, where you can learn more book-buying hints from actual experts. Continually educate yourself whenever you get a chance. You can do well in your new book-buying hobby with just the information in this book, but if you are so inclined why not expand your horizons and learn more as you go?

Dust Jackets
A first edition book by a renowned author can demand a good price, but get one with the dust jacket and you are in a great position, even if the jacket is worn and/or torn or in otherwise terrible shape. Collectors are funny people; they want the dust jacket almost as bad as they want the book. Remember that hardback books are somewhat resilient; they rarely get thrown away and are often well taken care of. Dust jackets, however, often get thrown out and damaged; thus, they are very much in demand. In a collector's eyes, a book is not complete without its dust jacket. Don't pass up on older antique or near antique books that do not have a dust jacket; many older books never had one to begin with.

Vintage Paperbacks
Some collectors seek out older vintage paperbacks. Their pages usually have an aged brown or yellow color. Many of these collectible books are from the fifties and sixties, and you will note that they are typically found with the same theme and/or author. Examples would be those cheap kind of romance, western, science-fiction, or detective novels, and so on. This could be a great find for you.

Any Book That Has Some Kind of Protection
Occasionally you will find a book, generally hardbacks but paperbacks sometimes too, that are protected in some kind of plastic or even wrapped in cellophane wrap. Why were they protected? Don't even hesitate; just buy it. Someone for some reason felt this book should be more protected than normal. Sometimes it's nothing, but sometimes there could be high value for that book, and the prior owner knew it.

Yearbooks

I buy any high-school or college yearbook I find, but will not pay more than five dollars, preferably much less. Although it may seem that the older yearbooks would hold more value my opinion is that there could be a challenge to that: little demand. If the yearbook is too old, and all those young kids in the photos are no longer with us, then who's going to be interested in the yearbook? Whereas if the kids in the photos are still alive then of course there is more demand. There are exceptions of course, for instance some old yearbooks (and the newer ones for that matter) have students that became celebrities or even presidents. This can be a bit time consuming to research, but perhaps something fun to do on rainy day.

In general, yearbooks are the type of item that may take a while to sell because of the limited demand, so you will need to be very patient. If they just do not sell in a reasonable period of time, you can always bulk sell them. Selling yearbooks is one of my favorite items to sell because I feel I have been able to bring back a special memory into someone's life. Sailing is not just for you; it helps other people!

Magazines

There is a demand for back issues of magazines, but be careful; many back issues are worthless, so you should familiarize yourself with the kinds of magazines that will sell. Doing so will save you a lot of headaches and backaches—magazines in large quantities can be very heavy! Do some checking for closed auctions; you will slowly begin to become a back-issue magazine expert. You can even make a cheat sheet to carry with you. Put the names of the magazines on an index card in a small font and in alphabetical order. When you see a stack of old magazines sitting in someone's garage, take out your index card and see if it's on there. If it is, buy it; if not, skip it. You want to make sure that what you have is a resalable item because it is a bit more labor intensive listing multiple items like this. You will have to item-ize each one with the year, date, and volume number. You can still do it quite fast, but why spend any time or effort at all if there's a good chance they will sell for very little or not sell at all?

Magazine collections, similar to book sets and unlike individual books, can be checked quickly on your smartphone right there at the sale; just type in the magazine name along with the word *lot*. For example *lot of* Time Life *magazines 1970 to 1980*. If very little or nothing comes up they take the word *lot* out and see if that produces some results. You will immediately have an idea of value, a very good thing before having to lug heavy boxes to your car.

So now, for the purposes of this book, you are an amateur book scout! Trust me, you probably just received more education in thirty minutes or however long it took you to read this section, than most people who attend garage sales ever learn. The question you have to ask yourself is what to do with collectible books. As we referenced at the beginning of this chapter, Amazon has certain restrictions and approval is needed to sell collectible books. For me personally, I will typically keep these books and add them to my collection. If I do sell them I use eBays auction or fixed price format depending on the indi-vidual book but even then, it's very important to stay on top of auc-tion house rules. For instance eBay does have conditions if you are selling an autographed book. But again, for me, selling collectible books is rare, I typically hang onto them.

You need to make a decision for yourself; consider starting a collection or if that does not interest you think about selling them on eBay as I do. You can also scout on-line and find perhaps other options to sell them, things are constantly changing so try to keep us with new options, not just for books but for anything you choose to sell on-line.

You may opt to simply bring them to your local used bookstore, which would be an easy and quick way to sell but perhaps not as profitable. Whatever you choose, rest assured you are eventually going to run across books that have collectible value and when you do I trust it will be an exciting find for you!

Format to Selling Books
So will you come home with boxes and boxes of books? Because of all the restrictions set forth above, you are most likely going to have fewer books than you might assume. For me? I generally come home with two or three banker-style boxes of books, books that I feel will sell well on Amazon that is. The only exception occurs if I choose to play the old-book or even modern-hardback first-edition slot machine. If that's the case, I will have quite a few books! But for the sake of keeping this simple, let's say you come home with two or three boxes of about fifty potentially Amazon-worthy books, that is, general, non-collectible books. I've put together a system for you to very quickly go through them and discern value. It's very similar to the CD-selling process with a few differences. Here it goes.

I have my own personal system. You can use it or tweak it around your own ideas, but here's the system I have found to be the most productive, profitable, and time efficient.

Amazon (Reread Chapter 1, Section "Why I Use Amazon")
Always read Amazon's rules and guidelines and keep up with the changes; that said, become an Amazon seller. It's easy to join, just like eBay. You can sell just about anything on Amazon, but for the purposes of this section, we are going to refer to books only.

Selling Merchant Fulfilled Network (MFN)
If you choose to sell through MFN, you will need to look at what the non-Prime prices are and see if your books are worth listing. There is no right or wrong answer. Again, I do not sell through MFN, but if I did, I would want to make at least seven or eight bucks a book, plus shipping, to make the selling worth my time.

Selling Fulfilled by Amazon (FBA)
In my opinion, FBA is the only way to go. Once you have listed and shipped the books to Amazon, you're done. Aside from inconsequential things like checking my competition or lowering my price, you do nothing but wait for the money to show up in your bank account. I mean *nothing*. You don't do shipping or handling. You don't deal with the buyer. You don't deal with returns. You don't deal with packaging items—nothing! We are going to move forward in this section as if you were selling FBA.

Enter Barcode or Title into Amazon's Seller System
So now you have those two or three boxes of books. Even though you have been very choosy in what to buy, not everything is going to be salable, but the more you do it the less of those books you'll be bringing home. Regarding the two or three boxes of books, I can pretty much bet that out of all that you will end up with at least one full box of very salable books to send to Amazon.

Type in the barcode on the book (or you can buy an inexpensive scanner that reads barcodes for you) You'll know the barcode when you see it. If there is no number then just type in the title of the book. Once you type or scan (do consider buying that scanner, they are so easy to use and inexpensive and will save you so much time!) that item will usually pop up.

Check the Lowest-Offer Price with Your Same Condition
Since you are selling FBA, check "Prime Members Only" prices in your search. When you see that the Prime members are being offered a certain price for your exact book in similar condition, check that price and see if it's within your comfort zone then list it! Just try to describe the books as carefully as possible. I must add, however, that everyone's comfort level could be different. For me personally I would want to net at least five dollars per book after all costs to make the process worth it. However, if I have already gone through

the process of scanning and checking and I see that I will only net about three dollars, I'll probably still do it. Why? Because I have already gone this far in the process so what the heck. That said if I knew beforehand that I would net that little, I simply would not move forward in the process. But do be aware of all costs; remember books are heavy, and although you will be utilizing the most inexpensive way to mail, it's still something to take into consideration. The amazing thing is that many of the books you find will sell in a higher range—well into the twenty-dollar-plus range—all for an investment of maybe a buck!

Amazons Tools
Among other tools available, Amazon has a wonderful feature wherein you put your item title or barcode in and it will break down the cost for you so you will know before you list it how much you are going to make. After a while you will get to know the type of items that will yield a decent enough profit and not have to check each and every time.

Tough-Selling Books
Amazon will let you know if your item is going to be a tough sale prior to you completing the listing. I figure they know what they're talking about, so I almost always adhere to their advice and do not proceed with the listing.

Online Sites That Will Buy Your Unwanted Books
I really don't like to go this route because I would rather deal directly with a local used bookstore, but if you are so inclined, there are online companies that will buy some of your books. See appendix.

Sell on eBay
It is something you can look into. I will occasionally sell collectible books or a collection of books or magazines on eBay; other than that

it's very seldom I use eBay to sell my general non-collectible books. I personally prefer utilizing Amazons FBA for that.

Unwanted Books Sold by Genre

If I have a grouping of books in the same genre, then sometimes if the price is right, I will bulk sell them on eBay. Let's take poker for example. Individually some of these books might not sell well; however, get a dozen or so books on how to play poker and you'll probably get an enthusiast or wannabe poker professional who will bid. The same can go with any genre, sports, hobbies etcetera. You can even sell bulk books of the same author, as mentioned earlier in this chapter.

Loser Books

So then what happens to all the leftover losers books? Donate them? Not yet! They stay in those banker-style boxes and get put somewhere out of the way. Once you have accumulated enough to fit in your car, call on your local used bookstore and make an appointment to bring them in. Most used-bookstore proprietors will *not* be happy with you showing up at their door with a dozen or so boxes of books, so do make that call first. Tell them how many boxes you have; most importantly, tell them the boxes of books consist of a bunch of mainly nonfiction trade paperbacks. Use that *exact* phrase, and I'd be surprised if they refused an appointment for you to bring them in. If you're lucky, they are the type of proprietor who will evaluate the books quickly, in about an hour or so while you wait; otherwise, you might have to leave the books at the store for a day or more and come back later, which is somewhat a pain. I won't leave my books in such situations; I just don't have the time. Just make sure you find out before you haul them all down there.

If the proprietor offers cash and you would rather take that than credit then do so. Otherwise, if the bookseller does not offer cash or they do and you really don't need it, then I would strongly suggest you start a rare-book collection. Take the credit. It will typically be much higher than the cash on offer. Once you have saved enough, buy yourself a rare book, something on a subject you enjoy. I would typically wait until I had $1,000 or more in credit so that I could purchase a rare book. At any rate, once the buyers have finished evaluating your books, take the remainder of them to a second bookstore if you are so inclined or if you do not want to do more hauling around then just immediately drop them off at a donation store, but do it right away so you do not have to unload and reload them back in your car. At that point, once you have left the books at a donation center, the book-buying process starts all over again—how fun!

Develop a Business Relationship with Your Local Used Bookstores

Do you want to take the used bookstore thing a step further? For those of you with a bit more time on your hands, here's a great way to earn extra money or start a rare-book collection. I did this for years, and as a result I currently own a beautiful and quite extensive collection of books, including a copy of the aforementioned *Carrie* by Stephen King *with* the dustjacket! For those of you choosing to do this, do everything listed in this section, except for the books I told you *not* to buy. Buy them, unless you see the majority are in bad shape; then walk. But if they do look mostly good, buy them, all of them—mass-market paperbacks, trade paperbacks, hardbacks, and older books. But keep the Amazon books I instructed you to buy separate from the "do not buy" ones. The only exception would be if you chose *not* to do the Amazon thing; then you could just mix them all together. You will amass a large collection of books extremely fast. I must strongly advise you, however, that since you are buying the entire lot, you had better get one heck of a deal, none of this buck-a-book thing! Trust me, you are doing the proprietors one huge favor; remember, come the end of the sale they're going to have to haul all those heavy books away. They will most likely be very tired and weary after being up all night preparing for their sale, and they've been in the sun all day dealing with hordes of people; they are often just simply exhausted.

Let's say I saw two relatively big boxes of books, maybe one hundred in total, I would just tell the sellers I'll take them all off their hands for twenty bucks. I might go a little higher or even lower for that matter depending on the subject matter. Now, if I saw ten boxes of books totaling close to five hundred, does that mean that I would offer one hundred dollars since I was willing to offer twenty dollars for one hundred books? No, not at all. I would probably offer very much less than one hundred dollars then will work my way up to that number if I deem it appropriate. The more I have to carry away, the lower the price should get. It will typically work; if not, make a judgment call, but really try to avoid paying too much unless you see lots of potential winners in great condition. Typically for these types of sellers, it's not really so much about the money than it is getting the books the heck out of their yard.

Okay, now that you have amassed all these books, what next? You can do one of two things. Stop buying once you have enough boxes to fit in your car. Then proceed to make an appointment with your used bookstore for an evaluation, or if you are so inclined and have the room, such as half of a garage you never use or a shed, just store the books. You will have oodles of books in no time, but only do this if your local used bookstore will agree to come to your home to check and make an offer. If this is the case, once they are finished, have a second used bookstore come out and do the same thing; often one bookstore's rejects are another bookstore's needs. Once the second store has been out, call a donation center, and ask them to come pick up your books. If they say no, call another. I can almost guarantee you one of the many donation stores out there will be more than happy to pick these up for you.

One huge perk to buying almost all the books you see is that you are hugely increasing your odds of coming across books that are rare, valuable, and sometimes even signed by a famous author. You will almost for sure find books that you want to read. Have fun buying books, and let yourself enjoy the hunt, the selling, and the book-store trading if you so choose. It can be an awful lot of fun and quite lucrative.

One last thought as we end this chapter. Just as I brought up online sellers who do well selling CDs in quantity and making a little for each CD sale, the same holds true for books, perhaps even more so. You can do very well selling books online for low amounts; it's for sure a numbers game just like with the CDs. Look into it; this could be something that might be suited for you. The options in garage sailing are limitless!

So there it is, an assembly line of sorts to extract as much profit from your books as possible.

9
Marketing Your Finds

THE TIME IS about three o'clock on a Saturday afternoon. You have just pulled into your driveway with a carload of new finds. Normally, you would be tired as you have gotten out of bed early and have been driving around for a number of hours; contrary to expectations, however, you're quite pumped up because you cannot wait to discover what kind of treasures you have. This is the essence of your sailing hobby—enthusiasm. Bringing my finds home is typically one of the most exciting elements of my sailing experience. I can actually see the fruits of my labor. In this chapter, you will learn what to do with your items from the time you bring them home to the time you mail them out.

Researching Value

When you hear the word "research," you may envision loads of paperwork and hours of time or, perhaps, such things reserved for a scientist or historian. Research will be quite the opposite for you. This is a simple process when appropriate systems are in place, systems that will help you establish a general idea of value and how to price your items intelligently. For some of your finds, you will have an easy time discovering value or you may have already gotten it at the sale with your smartphone. For others, you may need to exert more effort.

In this section, you will learn how to discern your potential income quickly and what to do with certain items for which establishing value might be difficult. You will also learn what to do when research leaves you completely empty handed.

Using Your Online Auction House
eBay, for instance, has systems in place that practically do the research for you. You can find out current auction prices and closed or final bids. I prefer to check successfully closed auctions only. What other people are asking is quite irrelevant when trying to accurately estimate value. It makes more sense to find out what items ended up selling for rather than what people were trying to get for them. The only exception would be if there were no closed sales. In cases like this, I try to find active sales and keep an eye on them until the close of the auctions. Then if I see there was a trend of value, I list the relevant item at a similar closing price.

One side note, don't get too excited yet if you see your item sold for a very high price; make sure you see a pattern of that item selling for or near that price. Sometimes for whatever reason one sold for a huge price and the rest not so huge.

When checking closing-price information, you need to type in some keywords that the system will recognize. In turn, items that match those words will appear for your viewing. Here you will see the start and end prices, as well as how many bids there were for each item. Your search results will also show what items ended up unsold. Play around with your preferred auction-house system until you get comfortable with how it works. Narrowing down value by search is quite simple, but what you do with the information is another story.

An auction history provides information that establishes particular item's value, but you won't necessarily receive the same value for your similar item. The research only gives you an approximation that will help you price your item. The following sections cover other variables that come into play during the pricing game.

The Online Auction House Is No Help
You've looked and looked, and there's just nothing that compares with the item you are holding in your hand. At this point, start looking around the Internet. Do a Google search by typing in a general description of your item. You may find what you are looking for or perhaps a similar item is mentioned in someone's blog. (Blogs, in general, can be great sources of information!) But don't spend too much time conducting your research in this manner. If you are having challenges, online appraisal sites are available. You simply describe your item, upload some photos, and pay a nominal feel (around ten dollars), and in a few days, you'll get an appraisal e-mailed right to you. Using such sites is a great way to price your items; what's more, if you find something you want to keep for yourself, you can get a written record of its value through this appraisal site. Check the appendix for information on online appraisals.

Old Books
If you cannot find final value on old books you have found then I would suggest going to both Amazon.com and Abebooks.com. Check books similar to yours from the highest on down. If you see multiple copies of your books not sold but all asking relatively the same high price, then there is a chance you have a real winner.

Condition and Packaging of Your Particular Item
You must pay close attention to all of the particular attributes of your item *and* the items you are using for comparison; doing so is extremely important. Let's say you come across a rare find, an old vintage train set, the kind that kids get on Christmas morning. The young child of yesteryear that had received this thoughtful gift used it for about a month or so; then the child stuck it in a closet. Years passed, and the train came out occasionally during the holidays, but for the most part, it sat in that closet. Seventy-five years or so later, a grandchild or great-grandchild decided to liquidate "junk" from the house. You

luckily stumble across it on a Saturday morning and get it for a great price. When you get home and inspect it more carefully, you notice that in addition to this item being in seemingly great shape, the box containing it looks as though it had just came off a toy store's shelf!

It's time to do your research. You find a comparable model that sold for a decent price, so you move on to list yours. Unfortunately, what went unnoticed as you were doing your research is that the item you were using for comparison had no box and had missing parts. The difference in value between yours and the other is huge. You failed to observe crucial details of the item used for comparison, so you end up listing your item too low. During the week of your item's listing, fewer than normal train set buyers are out there, and someone ends up getting a heck of a deal with your train.

The situation could have gone the opposite way. Your low price could have been an attractive bait for a number of buyers who happened to be looking, resulting in multiple bids and a great ending price. But why take that chance? Don't waste time over researching an item, but still be as thorough as possible. You should price such items at attractive amounts but not ridiculously low. In my experience, I find that about 50–60 percent, give or take, of the value of an item is low enough to attract attention but high enough that if the item only receives one bid, I'll still be comfortable. There are many books and articles about how to sell items via online auctions. The above opinions are just my own; they have worked for me, but my preferences shouldn't prevent you from investigating others. My suggestion is just to "kick the wheels" until you feel comfortable with a system.

Names, Numbers, and Dates Printed on Your Item
You want to research more than just similar items. If possible, research your exact item. You will find that a great tool is a good-quality magnifying glass. Your being observant is one of the key factors to research. A botanist, for example, must be extremely aware of details. One fine and seemingly insignificant marking on a petal

of a flower could mean the difference between a rare, extinction-facing plant and a common wild flower. You, too, must be very aware of markings on your items, especially the antiques and collectibles you find. Let's say you find an antique bamboo fishing rod leaning against the wall of a garage, and you pick it up for ten bucks. You bring it home, do a little research, and find two or three similar look-ing rods that have sold for over fifty dollars—okay, not bad. You list it for twenty dollars, and the bids go up to fifty dollars. It's still a decent profit, because you made five times your original investment.

The buyer receives it in the mail a few days later and, after closer observation, sees a small name and number printed on it. This lucky buyer jumps jubilantly with the discovery. As an antique-rod collec-tor, he knows the one he just bought for $50 is worth at least $500; it was custom made by a short-lived fishing-gear maker from the early twentieth century. You obviously made a crucial mistake by not pull-ing out your magnifying glass and researching the item thoroughly before you compared it with its counterparts. Be aware of names, dates, serial numbers, manufacturers, copyright information, and the like.

Anything that will help distinguish your item from others is impor-tant. This way, when you are researching comparable finds, you can intelligently base the price not only on items that look the same but also on identical ones.

Uniqueness and Differentiating Features

In addition to printed or engraved information, certain features can help distinguish your items from comparable ones. This is a little more tedious to do. Small indentations or curves may go unnoticed. The best way I have found to perform this kind of research is to first enlarge the photos of comparable items. If possible, hold your items next to the enlarged photos and try to discern differences or similari-ties in the features. Second, carefully read and compare the descrip-tions of the other items to yours. Finding distinguishing features can be a bit more difficult than simply finding model numbers or names.

Avoid spending too much time at comparisons, but give them concen-trated efforts to eliminate any potential underselling of your finds.

Pricing Your Items
In the following section we are going to use round numbers. Often a seller will price an item for instance at $99.00 instead of $100.00. This is something you definitely want to consider doing but for the sake of easier reading we will simply refer to round numbers.

Now that you have narrowed down items that compare to yours in condition—looks, markings, numbers, and the like,—you can now move on to the next phase of your research: bidding history. What a wonderful tool as we referred to earlier in this chapter.

An Item Had No Bids
In such cases, the item might have been unpopular or priced too high, or the headline might have incorrectly matched the product or per-haps the seller placed it in the wrong category all together. Look for other similar items to see if any of them sold. If you see a trend of unsalability then your item may end up being worthless and that's okay. At least you are saving the time and money by not listing unsal-able items. In addition, you have just learned a valuable lesson of what to avoid buying in the future!

Sometimes, however, an item has value but just was not popular enough to get any bids, or the small population of interested buy-ers were not paying attention during the listing's lifespan. So never solely depend on an item's lack of bids as the sole determinant of value, but do be cognizant of trends of unsold items.

An Item Had Very Few Bids
Look to see if other similar items also had extremely low bids. If you see five or six had no bids and only one or two had a couple, under-stand that your item is walking a fine line between being worthy to list or not list. You may see that a higher percentage of similar items ended up selling, even though there were only one or two bids each

and that the prices are high enough to warrant your own effort in selling your item. In such cases, go for it. You are taking a chance that your item may not sell, but at least it is a thought-out, researched, and calculated decision.

An Item Had Multiple Bids
This is like someone waving a huge banner and saying "Winner!" The rule of supply and demand is definitely at work here and to your benefit; obviously, there are more buyers than there are items. The number of bids on an item can help calculate an appropriate starting price for your own. Let's say that you found an old clarinet in its original case. After thoroughly researching it, you found the exact same clarinet with the same manufacturer and model number. It was also in similar condition and ended up selling for $150. You then looked at the bid history, and there were only two bids on it. Obviously, out of all the clarinet buyers out there, only two people wanted this item, and now one of them has one. If you priced yours at $50, you would be leaving yourself open for one bid at $50. In this case, I would probably price it at about $75 to $100 and would be happy to get that. If I didn't, I could always lower the price on a relist. Keep in mind that new buyers are always surfacing, so my old clarinet might very well end up with more than one bid.

Let's look at another example. Say you found a vintage Tonka truck in absolutely beautiful condition. You did your research to find that similar trucks in close to the same condition had sold for about $250, and they had at least half a dozen or so bids on them. You are definitely in the driver's seat. You feel quite comfortable knowing that your item would sell for at least close to that. In this case, I would probably list the item for right around $150 to $200, give or take.

Some sellers would list it for the entire $250 or more, but I think they would be taking some of the excitement and challenge away from the buyers, which could result in fewer bids. On the contrary, some sellers would list it for $5. I think that would also be a mistake because of the obvious interest in this item. There would actually be a happy medium to selling this item: "Buy It Now."

Buying Formats

Buy It Now

This is exactly what it sounds like. It is still an auction format, however you are giving the buyer the option to forget about the entire bidding process and buy the thing right then and there; in doing so, they are wiping out any potential competition. The item, of course, cannot have any bids on it for this to work. That Tonka truck could be best listed as a Buy It Now item. Remember that these sold for about $250. Why not list it for $200 and put it at a Buy It Now price of $225? The buyer would get it $25 cheaper than the last one and would not have to worry about other bidders or waiting. The buyer could have that Tonka truck in his or her hot little hands in a few days, well before the auction ended. You just need to pick and choose which items work best this way. There is trial and error, but you will get the hang of it.

Fixed-Price Listings

There is no auction. What you are asking is what you are asking—period. I like using this on lower-priced items or things I know have a low likelihood of going over a certain price. I just price it at or a little below what similar items are selling for, so I get the sale faster, without having to wait for a bunch of bids. A lot of buyers only buy this way. They don't even want to deal with bidding and not knowing if they get the items or not, even if they have to pay a little more than they would in a bidding situation. To be honest, when I buy items on eBay, I typically look for the fixed-price and Buy It Now items first before I consider making a bid on an auction. Other buyers out there are doing the same thing. Putting an item on an auction that is better suited for a fixed price or buy it now format could very well hinder you from getting the best price possible and could even hinder the item from selling at all.

Best Offer

For the most part, personally, I don't like it. This gives a buyer the opportunity to give you an offer on an item lower than what you are asking. Let's say you have an item listed for one hundred dollars. If you advertise Best Offer, you will get people making silly offers. Yes, you can set it up where offers under a certain amount will get refused automatically, but foolish offers are irritating. This is my opinion only. I just don't like wasting my time with feeble, rather insulting offers.

But, are there exceptions? Yes! In my opinion, Best Offer can come in very handy under certain circumstances. Let's say it's an item you just know should have sold but did not. You did an auction for a week...nothing; Buy It Now for another week...nothing; Fixed Price for one more week and, still, nothing. Instead of just discarding the item, you can list it under Best Offer, and whatever you get (as long as it's somewhat within reason and worth your time) is better than nothing.

Also, if you found a one-of-a kind item in a category that may have a large price range, Best Offer can help it find its correct price. For example, Best Price can help you sell a collection of signed books from an unknown or very obscure writer. How do you price that? There are typically little to no guidelines to help you out depending on the obscurity factor, so you can start at a high price and hope that fans of that artist or even amateur collectors (who would be other-wise unable to afford the signed books of better-known writers) will make offers. Again, the Best-Offer format might help you find the unknown price. The item was on its way to a donation store anyway, or if you're like me and the item is compact and small enough like a few books, you can just store them away and maybe revisit selling them in the future or just keep them indefinitely. There may be some value or at least some clarity of value at some point in time.

Reserve Price
A reserve price is the minimum amount you are willing to take. In other words, someone might for example, price a one-hundred-dollar item for a dollar and establish a reserve price of fifty dollars, which would guarantee they do not have to accept a price lower than fifty dollars. I am sure there are auction experts who can write a book

on reserve pricing alone. Be that as it may, I simply do not utilize the reserve option; it has never made much sense to me and does not seem applicable to my level of business.

I have a few pricing philosophies. There are many schools of thought on this topic. Just like with the aforementioned reserve auction expert, there are also online marketing and sales experts, as well as accountants and financial analysts, who could run circles around me with their knowledge on pricing, buyer psychology, and marketing. My reply to the fact that there is so much knowledge and expertise out there is to *never* forget that you have entered into this endeavor to make money *and* have fun. If you choose to get more serious about it, there are dozens of books and seminars available that can lead you in certain business directions that I cannot. My goal is only to make the process easy, fun, and profitable. I have found that pricing the way I do just works well for me. You have to become comfortable with how you choose to proceed. More than anything, I use my gut reaction and past experience in establishing attractive starting prices. I feel being too analytical can take up unnecessary time and energy. You have to make the decision for yourself and proceed in a manner that you feel is appropriate.

Writing a Description That Sells
You have done your research and established a fair starting price for an item. It is now time to put it up for auction. Pick up the newspaper or go online and check out the real estate sections. Read some of the ads that describe homes for sale. You will note that the wording is more than a description of the property. For example, let's take a three-bedroom, fifteen-hundred-square-foot house built in 1925. It still has its original hardwood flooring. Technically, the ad could read using the above information, but it most likely will not. Rather, it will read something like this: *a lovely and vintage three-bed charmer with a spacious floor plan and beautiful hardwood flooring, just waiting for you on an inviting, tree-lined street.*

The same thing has been said, but the house has been made into a home. You will be doing similar things with your items. Let me emphasize that under no circumstance should you ever mislead or tell untruths. You should describe items in ways that are compelling *and* accurate.

Headlines

There is so much information available online about hints on how to write headlines or really hints on practically everything related to listing an item. That said, here is some basic information I think you will find useful.

Just as headlines attract viewers to read a particular article, so will your headlines be a useful tool to get buyers' attention and to compel them to investigate your items further. The type of headline I'm referring to is the one-sentence overview, which is the first thing the potential bidder reads. eBay also has a subtitle section available for a fee. This may be something you would want to invest in for an item that simply needs more headline space, especially with higher-end auctions. It is amazing how much information you can give with just a few words. This is where being creative is important. Use keywords that will jump out at the reader: *rare, original, hard to find, clean, possibly never used*, and so forth, are powerful words and phrases to implement. Don't be afraid to use your imagination, but don't misrepresent your items. Also, ensure you use keywords that pertain directly to what you are selling; doing so will widen search results for interested buyers. If you have a vintage McIntosh stereo receiver (some McIntosh stereo equipment is highly sought out), for instance, make sure you use the name *and* model number of the unit, because many buyers are looking for very specific items. eBay and Amazon have great learning programs; use these tools to help you promote your items more accurately and effectively. The following paragraphs provide some hints that will help you make the headline-writing process easier.

Other Auctions
Look at other auctions that have resulted in profitable sales. Successful people share a common trait: they can put their egos aside, which allows them to observe and learn from other people's successes. If there are two auctions you are looking at for the same item and one ended up selling for a higher bid, try to craft your headline more like that one.

Wording
Use your words sparingly. Say all you want in the full-description category of the listing, but in the headline, pick and choose carefully. List the facts but express excitement about your items at the same time. Adjectives are good, but too many of them will look phony; they may even hinder you from describing your items accurately.

Name and Model Numbers
Use model numbers and names whenever possible. Collectors love and really need to know which model in particular you are selling if they are going to bid. I have found that depending on the circumstances, putting the serial number is not typically necessary, especially if there is a model number available. Sometimes your items will not have a model written on them, but that's okay. Just put down anything that will help describe the item. Of course, if there's any kind of name, definitely use that in conjunction with the model number. Keep in mind, the buyer is typically the real expert here, not you. Most likely they'll probably know more about what you have than you do. Your job is to give them the facts and as much information you can to help them piece the puzzle together so to speak; that's why earlier I suggested to ask the seller about the item and its history.

Here are three headline descriptions for a vintage suitcase, so you can see what I am referring to:

"Old Gucci suitcase with flower patterns and silk lining, good condition"

"Absolutely beautiful vintage Gucci suitcase with lovely and attractive flowered patterns"

"Vintage Gucci suitcase #123, with colorful flower pattern and silk lining, key included!"

Let's analyze each of these. The first one is very drab; it's giving an accurate description but missing any kind of zest or excitement, like the house example before the change in wording turned it into a home. The second is overdoing it. The seller is trying to make more of the item than it is and, in doing so, is leaving out important information. The last one is a winning ad. It is mixing in excitement with important facts, such as the model number and that it has a key for the lock.

Your goal is to get potential buyers intrigued by the descriptive and enthusiastic wording, encouraging them to continue investigating your items. That is not to say that the first or second line of the above example will not attract any viewers, only that it is needlessly limiting the item from potentially higher visits. In the full description, this seller can go on to describe the suitcase in much more detail, listing not only the attractive qualities of the piece but also the flaws as well.

Although it is important to be positive in your headlines, sometimes it is necessary and appropriate to point out negatives. Most negative attributes of an item can be listed in the full description; at times, however, the negative is such a large part of what you are selling that it's important the buyers know before they move on. Let's say you are selling an older thirty-five-millimeter camera, the kind used prior to digital (by the way, there are a lot of them out there that have good value. Could this be a niche for someone who's into cameras or wants to learn? Of course!). It looks to be in great condition, but it's just the body with no lens. This is important enough to put in the headline, such as "Nice condition but body only."

The Full Description

Here you have the opportunity to write freely about your items. If the relevant headlines work, potential buyers will investigate your items more closely. The Full Description section is where you want to describe your items in great detail; include the positives and negatives. Let's continue with that vintage Gucci:

> *Vintage Gucci suitcase model #123 with popular flower pattern and silk lining! It measures approximately forty-by-twenty-five inches and is approximately eight inches deep. The lock and key is included, which we are very fortunate to have! The latch is a little worn but still works. There are no evident tears or stains, but it does show some normal wear due to its age. I do not collect this kind of thing, so I don't know exactly how old it is. All in all, a very nice piece, in my opinion but you may know better than I. Money back guarantee!*
> *Good luck bidding!*

The description can go on as necessary. Note that the first part is almost identical to the headline. I simply cut and paste headlines into the general descriptions to save time and then edit as I see fit. Now if there was more written information on this item, such as dates, addresses, perhaps a serial number, or a copyright date, I would reference such information depending on what I felt was necessary. Note that I mentioned the key in an even more excited manner than the headline. Many of these old pieces have missing keys, so finding one with a key is worthy of an enthusiastic mention. You will notice that my description was exciting but pretty much to the point. Potential buyers' attention is hard to hold, so I think it is important to mention as many details as possible without going overboard.

The Full Description is also an appropriate area in which to mention disclaimers. You should describe items as accurately as possible, but be careful not to overdo that too. In some situations if you start itemizing each smudge, ding, and scratch on an item that has dozens of them for example, then you might be writing a novel. Do your best to disclose what you can about your items to make the buying process fair and easy for buyers, but keep in mind that sometimes it's impossible to describe something completely. Disclose the obvious, but then you may want to add a phrase stating that an item has miscellaneous scratches and smudges. You may also want to disclaim that you have accurately tried to describe the item and have provided photos to help. Always read your auction house's rules, requirements, and suggestions. Doing so is very important with regard to listing and describing your items. I typically offer a money-back guarantee, so if the buyer discovered something they were not happy with, they are protected.

Photos
A picture tells a thousand words. Within the description section, you can upload and insert photos of an item. In some cases, CDs for example, there is sometimes a stock photo available so you do not have to use your own photos. Aside from situations like that, buyers appreciate lots of photos and angles. Some items may need only a few photos because they are pretty cut and dry. Other items will require more than just a few. In regard to the Gucci suitcase, there may be different angles, defects, the inside lining, model numbers, and so forth, that you would want buyers to see. In a case like that, photos are a perfect opportunity to help describe an item. Photos can aid a collector for instance, to differentiate one collectible or antique from another. If you know nothing about a certain item, say so in the description and let the photos do the talking for you. Photos can also make an item look either better or worse than it really is. Just do your best to ensure your photos are as clear as possible to the real thing. That, combined with an honest description, will make the selling process fair for both you and interested buyers.

Over time, you will become faster and better at writing both headlines and descriptions. If you utilize the methods I've taught you and are aware of how other successful sellers describe their items, you should have no problem at this.

Partnering with Retail Stores

Familiarize yourself with local stores that resell used merchandise. Sporting goods are a perfect example. There are some used sporting-goods stores that will buy your finds or give you trade value. I do this with probably 90 percent of the golf equipment I find. I take it down to my local used golf store, take credit, and then save enough for something I really want. Pawnshops can sometimes be a bit tough, perhaps because they don't specialize in any particular item unlike the afore-mentioned sporting-goods store. Test it out for yourself but I typically don't use them. Let's say you are into photography. I bet you could find a used-camera shop that would gladly take many of your finds off your hands. They may give you cash or perhaps a nice credit that you could use to purchase a nice high-quality camera for yourself or a loved one, or even a high-end collectible camera you can keep for investment!

What to Do with Unsold Items

Unfortunately, sometimes you will end up with a failed auction. You may find an item that you thought would make a profit, but it ends up seemingly wasting both your time and money. Note the word *seemingly*. You just learned a very valuable lesson, and relatively speaking, did it actually cost you that much time and money?

The question now is what do you do with this item. Relisting it is the most obvious choice, which would be appropriate in many cases. The following are some simple hints:

Check Your Visitor Counter

If only two or three people have looked at your item, you need to make a decision whether to relist. This is a judgment call because there are no hard-and-fast rules. Your decision depends on the item and your past experience, which comes with time. I usually relist this sort of item with either a Buy It Now, Fixed-Price listing, or Best Offer, as articulated earlier. I have already made the effort to upload the item. Why not take another crack at it?

Check Your Description

You may have incorrectly or inaccurately described your item or even perhaps listed it in the wrong category. Reread your headlines and descriptions. Compare them with other successful sales of similar items. This is a perfect time to rewrite or add more description and enthusiasm. I feel the most important of these two is your headline. Perhaps you need to add a word or two that will attract more buyers who are using certain search parameters to find similar items. This is also a perfect time to check your photos to see if you can sharpen them or change their angles. However, avoid spending too much time on this unless it's a higher-end item; I do not want this to become too much like work!

Check Your Pricing

This is the most important aspect of your listing. For the most part, you should assume that if an auction ends with an unsold item, it is probably because of the pricing. If you started high purposely to see what would happen, change the price. If you feel the pricing was accurate but, for whatever reason, there were just not a lot of buyers looking at that particular time, you should consider simply leaving the price where it's at, for the time being anyway.

If the relist still does not work, it's time to make a corporate decision regarding the potential of this particular item. Sometimes you are just going to have to pull your item off completely and walk away. Never look at such conclusions as failures; think of them as valuable lessons that will save you time and money in the future. The more lessons you learn, the more successful and fun sailing will be for you. Put these failed items in a big box marked "Donate." When you have enough stuff, bring the box down. It will go to good use.

10
Keep the Customer Satisfied

ALTHOUGH YOU ARE alone in your humble little office and thousands of miles away from buyers you'll never meet, you are still in the people business. A relationship has been formed once you've offered something for sale and another person has shown interest. There is absolutely no reason why that relationship should be anything but amiable, genuine, and *fun*.

Throughout this book, I have repeated that garage sailing, first and foremost, should be conceptualized as fun. Remember that you are not selling real estate, stocks, cars, or multi-million-dollar contracts. Rather, you are liquidating small and relatively inexpensive products that you find at garage sales. You're excited to sell your finds, and buyers are as excited to buy them. Selling should be an enjoyable and pleasant process for both parties, yet at the same time, it should be professional. This is still a business transaction that involves money.

In this chapter, you will learn how to interact with buyers and their sometimes quirky ways. You will learn how to make a buyer feel as if he or she is the most important person in the world to you, even though the purchase may be just a five-dollar item. You will see how easy it is to establish and maintain a great reputation, and you will learn how to enjoy doing it.

Establishing Goodwill

For our purposes the basic meaning of goodwill is to gain an established reputation and solid record. This translates to consumers having confidence in you as a businessperson, which results in their being comfortable while interacting with you. On eBay for instance, a feedback system is in place that helps to establish goodwill. The ratings are a review of services and products and how they were exchanged. Feedback systems like this create a sort of checks-and-balances system. If you have negative feedback, other people won't want to do business with you. On the other hand, with a positive feedback rating, you will be sought after as a reputable buyer or seller. This is a great motivating factor that should encourage you to handle yourself in a professional and businesslike manner. You want to do everything in your power to create nothing but a positive rating as opposed to a negative or even neutral rating. This is very easy to do, and creating this type of goodwill will also make the business of buying and selling all the more pleasurable for everyone involved.

Properly Describing Your Items

The cure is in prevention. By making sure your buyers are very much aware of what they are about to purchase, both the positives and the negatives, you are preventing any future conflicts or misunderstandings. In the previous chapter, "Marketing Your Finds," you learned how to list your items for sale and how to describe their assets and liabilities. By doing so, you ensure that in no uncertain terms, buyers understand what they are getting into. You must remember that buyers are purchasing something they have only seen photos of.

Think about it. When you go shopping, the traditional way is that you walk into a store, pick up an item you're interested in, feel it, look at it, and (if applicable) try it on. There would be no question as to what you are about to spend your hard-earned money on. And if for any reason you were unsatisfied with your purchase, chances are you could just take it back and return it for an exchange or for your money back.

This does not necessarily hold true with buying on the Internet. Sure, many sellers have refund policies, but it's not as easy as it sounds. Sometimes you have to pay to receive the item, and *then* after anxiously waiting for it to arrive, if you find you are unhappy with your purchase, *then* you must repackage the item and drive it down to the post office. Now there is another shipping fee that you or the seller must absorb, and *then* you still have to wait for a refund. Clearly the process is a hassle.

In most cases, the products your buyers are purchasing from you are used, collectible, vintage, or antique. Completely and thoroughly describing them can be a difficult (if not sometimes impossible) task. But you must at least show due diligence in attempting to make sure your customers have a clue as to what they are getting into. Buying on the Internet can be scary. Your job is to ensure interested buyers feel as comfortable and informed about your items as possible, without you spending too much time.

The Buyer's Duties: Payment and Shipping Instructions
You described an item as best you could, and an interested buyer has made the highest bid and won the auction. Now what? This is where you can eliminate confusion and misunderstandings before they arise. For example, eBay has a section for instructions as to what is expected of the buyer after having won an item. Take advantage of these types of systems. The following sections provide hints on how to instruct and educate buyers on what is going to happen.

Payment Instructions
Be clear that payments are due immediately or within a reasonable period of time. Most buyers will adhere to that stipulation. If a buyer does not, no big deal. Send the buyer a nice note via the communication system and ask when he or she plans to make the payment. Will it be within the next twenty-four hours or so? If the buyer cannot

pay right away, ask how long he or she needs. If the needed time is reasonable, just honor that. Otherwise, apologize that this transaction needs to be cancelled and that you both should amiably move in different directions.

Shipping Instructions

How and when will an item be shipped? This is important to the relevant buyer, who probably is extremely excited and eager to receive the new purchase. A shipping description should be built into the listing when you first put it on. Most buyers know where to look for the shipping and handling time. When a buyer does not do that or simply neglects to look and then complains that he or she wants the item faster, nicely tell him or her that you are sorry. Tell the buyer that you were clear about the time frame in the listing, and he or she is welcome to cancel if doing so is preferred. Buyers typically will not cancel; sometimes they may even offer to pay a higher shipping cost to expedite it. That's your choice. I rarely don't do it because I try to ship all my goods at one time and not make multiple trips to the post office...time management!

The Seller's Duties

Once you have received your payment, the duties reverse: it is now time for you to fulfill your end of the bargain. This is probably the easiest part of the entire process. You have received the money along with the address of the buyer. All you have to do is package the item and mail it through the shipping service you advertise. With that in mind, prior to offering any specific shipping service check out their rates and service and choose what is most appropriate. On eBay and Amazon, systems are in place that enable sellers to pay for postage and print out shipping labels at their homes. There is no hard-and-fast rule; you can do it the old-fashioned way and simply write addresses on your packages and take them to a post office within the next one to three days or however long you asked for. You can even get tracking information on each item you send, so you can know where your packages are at any given time and when your buyers receive them. Your job is done...unless a buyer claims never to have received an item or did receive it but was unhappy with it, which brings us to the next section.

Dealing with Difficult People, Situations, and Refunds

And everything was going so well! You found a wonderful item, placed it for sale, received a great bid, got paid on time, sent out the item when you said you would, but now there's a problem. Welcome to the public relation and diplomatic side of your new hobby. You will enjoy mostly smooth sailing, but occasionally you will run into rough waters—some kind of difficulty, confusion, or misunderstanding somewhere down the line. The following scenarios cover two of the most common problems (I like to call them challenges) you may encounter.

"Where is my item?"

This will be your most common complaint. People can be impatient. But don't be too hard on such buyers; remember that they are excited or in some cases really need their new purchases. When this complaint rolls in, you may see two different types of personalities emerge.

The first one is very calm and even apologetic about asking you. This buyer may say something similar to the following: *"Hi, I'm sorry to bother you, but I was wondering if maybe this item hasn't been sent yet? Thank you so much for your time, and again I'm so sorry to have bothered you."*

The second one is more insistent. This buyer may say *"I paid for this just like you asked me and still have not received it! What's the deal?"*

For the most part, you will probably see something more in the middle.

Some things are simply out of your control. After you send an item exactly when you said you would, there is nothing more you can do. If the tension continues, on eBay for instance, you or the buyer can open a case (not a big deal, although the word *case* conjures up visions of court rooms). It's a simple step that has been put in place to try to keep everyone happy. You can also have your items insured. Contact your local shipping service to inquire as to the process and costs. Insurance is quite easy to do and relatively inexpensive and, in some cases, would actually come with the postage you have to pay. Finally, I would encourage you to have a tracking number for your item; often they too come with the purchase of the postage. The only time I do not have a tracking number is if I am mailing out a very low-cost item like an inexpensive CD or DVD and I am not taking it to the post office but rather dropping it in the mailbox.

In the end, I always do my best to make buyers happy. If I am dealing with an inexpensive item, I may just refund the whole thing and tell them to keep the item when it arrives and that it is on me, just to prevent any more hassle. Or I sometimes put a time frame on the estimated arrival. Even though shipping is out of my control, I will tell a frustrated buyer to wait another two days. If the buyer does not receive it by then, I will refund a certain percentage off the purchase price. That will usually calm this kind of buyer down unless of course they never receive the item, but I have found that to certainly be the exception.

"This item is not in the condition I thought it would be!"
Many versions of this situation exist. Generally they are uncommon, especially if you have done your due diligence to describe and uploaded plenty of photos of your item. But this kind of situation does eventually come up. You must handle each case uniquely.

If a buyer is complaining about a negative attribute that I very clearly disclosed in the relevant item's description, I will simply tell him or her to reread the description and look again at the photos, and

I will say that I did mention the problem. Sometimes people just don't pay attention to the details. When this kind of buyer sees that I did show good faith in my description, he or she should have no choice but to calm down. But, if they bought it with a money-back guarantee of course I'll let them return it for a refund unless they bought it without the guarantee, and even then, I might still just let them return the item.

A situation like this is quite black and white, but what if a buyer's complaint falls within a gray area? Yes, maybe you described an item as best you could, but the buyer did not think so. There are numerous variations to this problem. You could respond in an uncooperative manner, but that would put a negative light on the whole situation. I always try to make these customers feel as though their complaints are welcomed and taken seriously. Sometimes (not always) I have to keep this kind of customer satisfied by accepting a complaint and/or making a refund even though I feel it is not 100 percent founded. I recommend listening to the buyer, try making some sort of deal, and show that you care about the problem. If you do, you will gain a happy customer who should give you a good review, and in the end, you will be way ahead of the game in many different aspects.

However, never allow yourself to be taken advantage of. If the problem a buyer is complaining about is obviously false or something he or she certainly knew about before purchasing the item, stand up for yourself if you feel it's appropriate and worth it. I must say, however, that almost all of the complaints that come to me are sincerely and honestly made, and I am almost always willing to make good on the complaint if I don't have to be overly unfair to myself. Also, I often try to make a deal to save myself a lot of time and frustration. Again, as previously stated, I may tell the buyer that I will give a full refund. Or I will let the buyer keep the item, but I will take a certain percentage off the listing price—that is, I may make them a lucrative deal. The type of deal I make depends mostly on the relevant item. If it's a relatively low-cost item (say, fifty dollars), I may just cut payment in half or whatever I feel is most appropriate to help balance the scales. If it's a very low-priced item and the buyer is still simply not willing to deal, I will often tell the buyer just to keep the item as my way of apologizing for the inconvenience. What I'm also doing is making sure I don't get inconvenienced further or receive negative feedback. You have to weigh everything case by case. Larger-ticket items are a different story. I just feel out each item—that is, I decide what to do depending on the context. But again, truthfully, if you have listed the item properly and have been clear about condition, used lots of photos, followed through with all the rules etcetera, then it really should not happen that often.

Feedback
Obviously you want to receive positive feedback as much as possible and for sure you want to avoid negative feedback. Adhering to some of my suggestions will help you do so. Remember positive feedback works both ways; if you were happy with your buyer give them a nice feedback remark, they'll appreciate it!

End-of-Chapter Thought
Some people can be difficult to work with; that's a fact. We see that in our individual lives when we deal with the general public, coworkers, and even our friends and family.

I believe there are two ways to handle difficult people. The first would be to put yourself at their level and argue with them. This may work well at times, since some people respond well to such aggression, but I highly urge you to avoid taking that route. Negativity has a way of spreading. It is extremely contagious, and even if you win a problem by behaving this way, in the end, it will just put you and them in a sour frame of mind.

The second and most fruitful way to handle people is to be empathetic to their problems. If you choose empathy, you will see things from your buyers' perspectives, and whether you agree with them or not, your empathy will put you in a positive, understanding, and optimistic state of mind. From this healthy vantage, you can proceed to handle just about any difficult person or situation that comes up. However, under very few circumstances must you give in when you feel your kindness is blatantly being taken advantage of. Be wise in your decisions. Be bigger than the other person. Most importantly, treat others as you would want to be treated. If you adhere to my advice in this section, your sailing hobby will become not only more enjoyable and fulfilling but also more lucrative in the end.

11
Time Management

IT IS VERY important that you define how you plan to implement sailing into your life. For me, it's simple. Sailing is a hobby with an income. I have written this book so that the time allotments are geared toward spending a sufficient number of hours working toward the enjoyment and maintenance of a hobby or relatively small business. You, however, may choose to look at it more from a larger business standpoint. That would be great and I would fully encourage it; however, it will most definitely result in you having to stretch out my time allotments and systems to a different level. Whichever way you choose, to enjoy sailing successfully, you *must* be aware of time, for yourself as well as your family and friends.

I know that you can be successful at sailing with a minimal number of hours per week. I think that's what I enjoy so much about it. I have fun, but sailing does not cut into or irritate other areas of my life—if anything, it enhances them. I am a firm believer that having some sort of distraction in your daily routine is quite an important factor to successful and healthy living. The unique element about sailing is that it's a hobby with an income—a rare combination. Most hobbies are quite the opposite—the cash flow goes out rather than in.

Keeping Track of Your Hours

Have you ever tried to keep an accurate balance in your checkbook, only to find that you are overdrawn? If so, it is more than likely you simply forgot to make a debit entry. Keeping track of your money is the same as keeping track of your hours. To stay on top of things and avoid spending too much time sailing, you must keep some kind of log, at least when you first start out.

Coming up with a comfortable allotment of hours entails the simple task of jotting down your start and end times, along with some quick notations about how much you accomplished during that segment. Eventually, you will begin to see a pattern emerging that is a true reflection of how much you can get accomplished within a specific timeframe.

Once you have established that pattern, you will no longer need to take notations. You should, however, still write down the time you start so you know when to stop. I try to do this, and it really helps me stay on schedule. In general, I used to just go into my office and start plugging away with no regard for the clock, but much more than an acceptable amount of time would always pass before I realized it. How do you know when to stop if you have no clue when you began?

How Long Does It Take?

How long the processes and systems take can be different with each individual. If, for example, you do not know how to type, then uploading items for your auctions will obviously take longer for you than it would for a typist. If you are inexperienced with computers, it's going to take you longer to do things—at first, anyway. You will surprise yourself at how fast you can learn certain things! My point is that each individual is going to need a different amount of time to perform the same tasks. That being said, the following is my breakdown of approximate time periods for different sailing duties. My breakdown should help give you a general idea of time investments.

Selling CDs and books on Amazon is not included in any of the following time breakdowns. Time involved in selling CDs and books on Amazon is relative to how much you have and how much time you need to describe each item. Let's say for twenty-five books and fifty CDs, I can do that in two to three hours or so and that includes everything from the time I scan the barcodes to the very end when I have packaged and labeled the box to Amazon.

Saturday Mornings
I start around seven thirty in the morning and end around one thirty in the afternoon. I obviously have an investment of approximately six hours.

Research
Researching the value of my items is usually done over the weekend. It will take about five to ten minutes per item, quite often less. It really depends on what I am researching. If it's something that needs a Google search or an online appraisal then of course it will take longer.

Much of this was already done anyway on my smartphone at the sale itself.

Inputting an Item
This will depend on your typing skills and the item you are inputting. I do type, and for the most part, I spend about five to ten minutes per average item.

Checking Auctions
This I do periodically and during the day. It's just doing a quick overview of where my bids are. Also this can be a very fun distraction for you throughout the course of a day. You can even set it up that you will immediately get alerted on your smartphone every time someone bids or wins your auctions. It can be a mini jolt of excitement during the tedium of the day!

Trips to the Post Office

This depends on the distance to your local post office, what time of day you go, and how crowded it is. I am only about seven minutes away from my post office, so that's approximately a fifteen-minute round trip, with anywhere from five to ten minutes in line and with the clerk.

This adds up a total investment of about a half hour. But recall as mentioned earlier in this book, there is another way you can go, and that is printing and paying for postage online. You shouldn't have to wait in line because you have already paid; this could save you a substantial amount of time.

Packaging Items

DVDs and CDs take me just a few minutes each to locate, put in an envelope, and adhere the relevant addresses. Other items will take longer, depending on the size, fragility, and so forth. The average time needed should be about five to ten minutes to package an average-sized item.

Total Time Investment

For me personally and depending on how many and what kind of items I found, I would say when I do go sailing on Saturdays that a weekly average investment of time is about ten to fifteen hours, and that includes my sailing time.

All of the above are approximate times for me, but if you keep a log, as I've recommended, time frames will begin to emerge, making it easier for you to establish how many hours you will need to spend to obtain the desired results.

How Much Time Should I Invest?

This is entirely up to you, your schedule, and your goals. However, judging roughly from the above time frames, you are going to need a minimum of approximately ten to twelve hours per week perhaps a bit more as you get better and start finding more treasures. Again, this does not include selling CDs and books on Amazon.

Staying on Schedule
Staying on schedule can be one of the most difficult things to do, especially when you first start. The following sections provide hints that should help you stay within your time limits.

First Things First
Your first priority is to keep your customers satisfied, as we discussed in the previous chapter. To accomplish this and still stay on a strict timetable, ensure that you always start with customer service tasks, such as answering questions and packaging items. These should always be a number-one priority.

Think Big
After you have taken care of your customers, you will then start inputting your finds onto the auction block. Start with your largest, most cumbersome items. They can often take longer to input, and you want to ensure you have enough time to finish what you start. An added bonus to starting with larger items is that once they are listed for sale, you can put them away somewhere so they don't take up valuable space.

Small and Speedy
Once the larger items are out of the way, you can deal with the smaller ones. Pick the items you think you can input within the amount of time you have left. If you arbitrarily pick anything to list, you may end up with something more time demanding, which will put you over your limit.

Save It for a Rainy Day and Time Investments
Making sure you spend only your allotted time is one thing, but what happens when you are faced with the problem of having too much time? In other words, you lack enough inventory to keep you busy. Although this problem will apply more to people who live in climates that often produce inclement weather that prevents Saturday

outings, it can happen to anyone. Perhaps you've had a few slow sailing experiences, or maybe you have had some personal or business obligations that have prevented you from your Saturday excursions. Whatever the case, such hindrances will obviously leave you with fewer items to sell. You can use this time to do research, or if you have some old inventory, you can address that. Perhaps you have a bunch of old books that you have not had the chance to check value on. You can always find something to do.

When you have a windfall Saturday and come home with a huge number of items, avoid the temptation of going over your allotted time. Your excitement may demand that you input everything, but just list what you can using the time you have and save the rest for slow periods or the aforementioned rainy days.

One strict rule that I follow, however, is that if I don't have something to keep me busy on a rainy or missed Saturday, then I simply take the day off, and I do not try to make up those skipped hours somewhere else. For example, just because I missed sailing last Saturday does not mean that I now have six extra hours to use during the week. Before I started following this rule, I quickly saw that my weeks were thrown off balance because of the injection of more hours from missed Saturdays. The same can be said even for your daily allotment of time. For example, if you allow yourself an hour per day to work on things and you miss one day, that does not mean you can work two hours tomorrow? The answer should be, depending on your own individual circumstances, no. Understand that by doing this, you would be allowing yourself to go off schedule, which will result in a disruption of your personal routines.

I want to be very clear that finding a schedule that works well is going to force you through quite a bit of trial and error. We are all different and have unique talents and propensities. What one person can accomplish in an hour may take someone else two hours. Be very patient with yourself, as well as observant—that is, watch how you work. Take my suggestion of keeping a log of how long something takes you to do. In little time, you will begin to find a rhythm that works to your benefit.

Finally, I must warn you that when you start your new hobby, you are probably going to have to invest more hours because you have to set up your office, familiarize yourself with the process, and get comfortable with what you are doing. Simply be honest with yourself and your family and friends. Be prepared that there may be a bit more time needed at the beginning. However, once you get the ball rolling, you will quickly learn to pace yourself with an acceptable schedule. When you find that you have firmly planted your feet on the ground and have established a hobby that's fun and profitable, you will find other perks to sailing, both personal and financial ones, which brings us to the final chapter, "Self-Improvement."

12
Self-Improvement

IF YOU HAVE come this far in the book then good for you! Obviously you are taking this seriously and thus I am confident you will be successful!

You have absorbed quite a bit throughout this book so understand that there is absolutely no way you will accomplish everything I've recommended in one shot. And you shouldn't, anyway. Embrace your new endeavor step by step and with the same enthusiasm you would have in doing anything that interests you. Besides energy, your enthusiasm will produce patience because you will be enjoying both the results *and* the process involved in producing those results. With enough time, you'll have your office completely ready, your systems up and running, your schedule intact and extra money in your bank or pocket! Until then, enjoy the newness of the learning experience. With that being said, this next section is an attempt to give you hints as to how you can make sailing not only a hobby but also an avenue toward a healthier and happier life.

How Seriously Should You Take This?
That depends mostly on your needs and intentions. If your finances demand that you make this additional income every month, you'll take sailing much more seriously than someone else who is just looking for extra fun money. Perhaps, as stated earlier in this book, you

want to take this to a higher business level. I say go for it. But, again, by doing this, you will be taking sailing a bit more seriously, which will necessitate your having to prepare for it properly.

How seriously you take this will dictate the level of enjoyment you will receive. Note that I referenced level of enjoyment rather than how much enjoyment. I feel as though anything positive we do in life will carry with it a different level of enjoyment. Someone who plays softball with friends on Saturdays and goes for pizza and beer afterward is enjoying himself or herself differently than a professional ballplayer trying to make their dream a reality. However, they are (or should be, anyway) each thoroughly enjoying themselves, but on different levels. Your enjoyment level of sailing will differ depending on your intentions. With that in mind, move forward with the full intention of making sailing a fulfilling endeavor, no matter what level you decide on; that desire will most likely become a reality. If, after a while, you find that the fun scale measures very low, I would then highly recommend you find another type of venture to pursue or maybe just find a niche or niches within the sailing umbrella. The bottom line is that you will most likely do well at anything you enjoy. On the other hand the opposite could ring true and you might not produce the positive results you are looking for if you do not enjoy what you are doing.

Hints on How to Make It Fun
Once you start getting wrapped up in the nuts and bolts of sailing, it is very easy to get sidetracked and forget that you are supposed to be having a good time. What follows are ten hints that will help you raise the fun scale.

Have a Saturday-Morning Ritual
Get up at a regular time. Have the same breakfast or stop at the same place for coffee and a muffin. Whatever your personal routine is, stick with it. You will find that this little ritual will become part of your Saturday sailing adventure and will help start the day off in a positive, familiar way.

Smile!

Smile, especially when walking toward a garage sale. Trust me; for the most part, the sellers will be smiling at you—these people are typically trying to have fun! The scene almost has a Norman Rockwell–type look to it. The sellers have been planning their sales for weeks; they are enjoying refreshments just like a picnic, and often their kids and/or friends are involved. For a large part, they're making some fun money. Most importantly, they are all working together. Let that enthusiasm spread to you. It's easy and contagious, especially the smiling part.

Engage in Small Talk

Why not engage in a little small talk with proprietors, especially if they're a bit slow? You may even make some new social contacts while you're at it as I referred to earlier in the book.

I must advise, however, to use your better judgment as to how much time you'll spend engaging in conversation. If you are an extroverted type, you may find that talking will take up too much of your valuable time. Be conversational but aware of the clock.

If you're more introverted, you can do one of two things: stay introverted and just do your sailing, or use this as a cool opportunity to come out of your shell. Do what is most comfortable for you—this is *your* time. If you would rather avoid talking to people, that's okay—avoid it!

Challenge the Tendency to Get Frustrated while Driving

You'll be putting in a decent number of miles in a short period of time. You are going to run into those frustrating traffic experiences with inept drivers. Just consider yourself on vacation from everything, including getting irritated and angry.

Keep an Eye Open on Stuff to Give Away

One of the most exciting parts of my Saturdays, as I referenced earlier in this book, is when I see something that I know a friend or family member would love to have. It is all the more enjoyable when I see how happy and grateful they are that I thought about them, even if I only gave them a CD or book of one of their favorite artists or writers. You may also occasionally come across an item that you can return to the original owner. Once I found a very old family Bible and was able to reunite it with the heirs—now that was pretty exciting for not only the family but myself as well!

Keep Your Other Eye on Stuff for Yourself
Yes, one of the advantages of sailing is that you can find neat items for yourself. Aside from obscure objects that you love but don't necessarily need, you will also run across things that you do in fact need or desire (or both) and had every intention of going out and buying at full price.

For example, I was always on the lookout for a nice leather jacket at a garage sale. I really did not want to pay retail for one, partly because they can be quite pricey, but also I liked the challenge of being able to find one on a Saturday, and find one I did! It retailed for $5,000; now that is one nice leather jacket! I'd been looking for a while and quite frankly if I had found a jacket that retailed for $500 to $750, I would have been elated. Sometimes sailing will not only bless you but will bless you abundantly. At any rate I was talking to this fellow from whom I had bought some nice shirts, and the subject of leather jackets came up. He went into his house and brought one out for me to try on; it fit perfectly. He said he had paid $5,000. I believed him and purchased it for $300. It's how much he asked. I didn't blink an eye or try to negotiate. I later confirmed with someone I know big into fashion that this looked indeed to be genuine and it easily would have retailed for that amount. (By the way, I think that jacket had been worn only once!)

Clothing is expensive. If you are okay wearing preworn clothes, the sky's the limit. I have a closet full of very expensive Tommy Bahama and other higher-end shirts that looked to be barely worn, and I only paid about a buck or so apiece for them. If you are not comfortable with preworn clothes, just look for those tags. There're plenty of clothes out there from Christmas and birthday gifts that have never been worn with the tag still on them. In such cases, you will have saved yourself a bundle of money—just another sailing perk. Perhaps you are into cooking and you come across a set of vintage Corning Ware or perhaps a set of William Sonoma copper cookware, only a few years old and barely used, that retailed for over $2,000. What a great day you'll have buying something like this that you (and in this case your family) will personally enjoy. The list of course of things you can purchase for yourself can be virtually endless.

Find Brand New Items for Christmas and Birthday Gifts
Often you will come across a brand-new or never-opened item that would be absolutely perfect for a Christmas or birthday gift. Hold on to it; you'll get your holiday shopping done early, and you'll also save an awful lot of money! Oh and *shhhhh*. No one needs to know you found it at a garage sale!

Make Friends with the Postal Clerk
You'll be seeing the folks who work at your post office or mail house on a regular basis, so you may as well enjoy a little friendly chatter while you're at it.

Involve Your Family
Your kids or friends, for example, may want to help out a little—let them. If someone close to you shows a desire to hang out with you while you're packaging items or uploading auctions, look at that as an opportunity to do a little bonding. That said, I would recommend not taking them with you on Saturdays; that could be very distracting and will likely take you away from what you are supposed to be doing.

Brag!
Yes, one of the more enjoyable facets for me is owning the bragging rights to garage-sale stories. I shared a few of them in this book!

Perhaps you will pay five dollars for something that will make you a couple thousand or even much more! (hint; don't bring this up while at a nice dinner, everyone may expect you to pay!) Perhaps you will come across a beautiful antique desk for a song that ends up proudly sitting in your office. Perhaps you will find a painting that lacks financial value, but you hang it on a wall because you find your enjoyment of viewing it priceless. Whatever the case; if you're proud of one of your sailing accomplishments, don't be shy. Brag about it. Maybe you will excite someone enough to go out and buy my book!

Conclusion

Life has its ups and downs at times, which can be somewhat stressful, we all know this. I have found that sailing has added a dimension to my life that carries with it not only a distraction but also a sense of accomplishment and productivity. When I first was contemplating getting into this endeavor, I was a bit indecisive. I was worried I just did not have the time or energy to add something new like this to my life.

Then a good friend of mine said to me, "Let me ask you a question. How much time do you spend watching television each day?"

That's all I needed to hear. My friend was absolutely right, and off I went on a new hobby that has, among other things, brought me extra spending money, expanded my music and reading interests and historical education, encouraged me to forge new acquaintances, and, yes—you guessed it—allowed me to have *fun*!

I hope you too will find the same level of enjoyment that I have. The weather is perfect, and the winds are steady. It is time for you to set sail and seek new adventures out on the horizon.

Enjoy!

Appendix

Below you will find websites and references that I have used in the past. I am not endorsing any particular company over another. If you search, you should find many companies that offer similar services. These are just the companies I have used in the past with successful outcomes.

www.eBay.com: Who would not recognize the name eBay? It almost defines on-line auction houses. It's easy to set up an account and very tutorial in helping new sellers get started.

www.amazon.com: Just as the name suggests this is an AMAZON of a company. We are very fortunate to have this entity for both our selling and buying needs. Like eBay it is very user friendly and very eager to help those who desire to become sellers.

www.powellbooks.com: This is an online company that will buy books.

www.valuemystuff.com: This is a great online appraisal site. For a very small fee, you can get your item appraised by an expert in the relevant field.

www.abebooks.com: This is a great way to find out if you have a rare book on your hands. You can easily do an advanced search by author and title and then search by highest to lowest price, giving you a quick idea as to value.

A Pocket Guide to the Identification of First Editions, by Bill McBride: This is a great little pamphlet to have by your side when you have a book that you need to discern whether it's a first edition or not.

CPSIA information can be obtained
at www.ICGtesting.com
Printed in the USA
LVHW02s2345060318
568948LV00007B/243/P